Planning from Lesson to Lesson

A way of
making
lesson
planning
easier

Pilgrims

**Tessa Woodward
and Seth Lindstromberg**

Longman Group Limited,
Longman House, Burnt Mill, Harlow,
Essex CM20 2JE, England
and Associated Companies throughout the world.

© Longman Group Limited 1995

This book is produced in association with Pilgrims
Language Courses Limited of Canterbury, England.

First published 1995

Set in 10/12pt Cheltenham Book

Printed in Malaysia

British Library Cataloguing-in-Publication Data

A catalogue record for this book is available from
the British Library

ISBN 0 582 08959 X

Text Acknowledgements
We are grateful to the following for permission to
reproduce copyright material: Ewan MacNaughton
Associates for the article 'Police unlock riddle of
missing boot boy' by Paul Stokes in the *Daily
Telegraph* 5.10.93; the interviewees, Sheelagh Deller,
M.P. Harding, Pierre Jeanrenaud, Mario Rinvolucri &
Sarah Shaw for interviews.

Illustrations by
Kathy Baxendale and Chris Pavely

Author Acknowledgements

We would like to thank Mario Rinvolucri for comments on the earliest
draft of this book and an anonymous reader and the Longman crew
for comments on a later draft.

Certain portions of this book relate to articles we have written in
the past. The germ of *Echo dialogues* and *Variety dialogues* first
appeared in Woodward 'Spontaneity training' MET 1986/87 winter.
Teaching definition skills is an expansion of Lindstromberg
'Vocabulary learning and defining', Practical English Teaching, (1987)
7/4:43–4. Elements of *Stress posters/Vocabulary posters* derive from
Woodward 'Vocabulary posters' MET 1988 spring, and from
Lindstromberg 'Schemata for ordering the learning and teaching of
vocabulary' ELTJ (1985) 39/4:235–43. *Mapping* is an expansion of
Woodward 'Mapping the day' The Teacher Trainer 1989 3/2. The
ancestor of *Classroom dictionary* is Tessa's article of the same name
in MET 1985 summer.

A letter from the Series Editors

Dear Teacher,

This series of teachers' resource books has developed from Pilgrims' involvement in running courses for learners of English and for teachers and teacher trainers.

Our aim is to pass on ideas, techniques and practical activities which we know work in the classroom. Our authors, both Pilgrims teachers and like-minded colleagues in other organisations, present accounts of innovative procedures which will broaden the range of options available to teachers working within communicative and humanistic approaches.

We would be very interested to receive your impressions of the series. If you notice any omissions that we ought to rectify in future editions, or if you think of any interesting variations, please let us know. We will be glad to acknowledge all contributions that we are able to use.

Seth Lindstromberg
Series Editor

Mario Rinvolucri
Series Consultant

Pilgrims Language Courses
Canterbury
Kent
CT1 3HG
England

Seth Lindstromberg

Seth began teaching EFL in Japan after deciding to postpone turning his British Columbia teacher's certificate into a job in a junior high school. Several jobs and countries later, he now spends most of each year working for Hilderstone College in Broadstairs while doing some administrative work for Pilgrims in Canterbury. He has published a couple of dozen articles in various European and international EFL and applied linguistics journals. Tessa and he are married.

Tessa Woodward

Tessa was brought up in Devon and South Wales and took a degree at London University. She spent several years travelling, working in bars and restaurants and in more respectable jobs at the National Union of Students and in the Martin Luther King Foundation before switching to EFL in the mid-seventies. She is author of *Loop Input* (1988 Pilgrims), *Models and Metaphors in Language Teacher Training* (1991 CUP) and *Ways of Training* (1992 Longman, in this series). She has edited *The Teacher Trainer* (Pilgrims) since 1987, being its founder editor, and has published extensively in ELT journals generally. She has run a repeating British Council Specialist Course for teacher trainers and was the founding coordinator of the IATEFL special interest group for trainers.

Dedication

To Ann, Cynthia, Mona, all the nursing staff at 'A1 Neurology',
Oldchurch Hospital, Romford and all the friends and family who
kept us going throughout Tessa's illness.

Contents

PART 2 TEACHER THEMES: WAYS TO VARIETY

Introduction

Planning what to do in your next lesson can be a bit of a chore, especially if you're an inexperienced teacher. Even with thorough pre-service training, beginner teachers starting their first job may experience a sense of real panic when faced with planning just one lesson, never mind a whole week of lessons.

	Mon	Tues	Wed	Thurs	Fri
Class 1 9.00–10.30					
Class 2 11.00–12.30					
Class 3 1.30–2.30					
2.45–3.45					

Figure 1 An EMPTY (Gulp!) timetable for one week (the first of many)

After carefully writing 'Coffee', 'Lunch' and 'Tea' in the appropriate parts of an empty timetable (see Fig. 1), a sense of foreboding can set in as the teacher realises that somehow all the rest of that space has to be filled in too. Not only on the paper (for their director of studies) but also *with the students in the classroom*. The thought is often, 'What on *earth* am I going to do?'

We asked around to see how some very experienced teachers tackle the task. Here and elsewhere in the book we include bits of what some of them said. We're *not* suggesting though that everyone has to do what they do, we just want to begin to show what some of the main issues and choices are in planning lessons and sequences of lessons.

Here's one very experienced teacher who is often in the unenviable position of having to plan lessons *extremely* fast:

'I do a lot of stand-in. When people fall ill or don't turn up, I cover for them. This is *immediate* planning. You have about five minutes before you go in. I have a look at the file to see what the last teacher's done. But often there's no time for that. So, I'll do something that I've done before – a whole lesson – that I feel happy with. I could teach that whole lesson (to different groups) hundreds of times. I have an unlimited capacity for boredom! [laughter] No, it's not really that! It's that I can always concentrate on something different each time even though it's the "same" stock lesson. I can concentrate on the students and what they're interested in, not on the materials. Or I'll write down the students' language verbatim and then write them out correction slips. Or I'll tape-record some of the students and target something. For example, I'll ask the students to listen to the tape and look for errors in an area that they've done before. Then there's always the personal content that the students bring to the lessons: their personalities, problems and lives. Supposing I've set up some sort of moral debate, the students have to come to a consensus in twos, and then in fours, about a particular situation. The *form* of the lesson may be the same one I've used over and over, but the *content*, the ideas, the debate will be different.

'So, a "stock lesson" has a different feel each time you use it. In fact, it gets better the more you use it. You don't have to think so much about the steps, the materials – the motor side. You don't have to think so much about what you're doing. Your higher forces are released. It's like when you're learning tennis. At first you have to think about how to hit the ball and where to step, etc. Once you've got the hang of that, your higher mental forces are freed to think about the strategy of the tennis game. So with teaching. Once you've taught a lesson a time or two, you're freed to think about whatever comes up from the students' side. If you always teach new lessons, you're so busy thinking about what you're doing that you never have a chance to just go in and learn.'

A teacher of about fifteen years' experience

Using stock lessons, with a new slant each time, is one excellent way of dealing with a very difficult planning situation. What do other experienced teachers do when they have more time than the teacher above has? Here's someone else talking about her Monday class:

'Let's say I have a class next Monday morning. Actually, I *have*! On Sunday afternoon I vaguely mull it over. I think about what we've done this term so far. It's the last week of term next week too so they're a bit jaded, low-energy. I don't want the last week just to trickle out though. I want to end on a high so they go away feeling good. I know it'll be tricky. So I mull it over. Then I leave it to simmer. That evening I'll go to bed and an idea will pop up. It could be an activity that I haven't done with them, or a language area, anything, really. I go to sleep thinking about it. Next morning it'll be there. If it's something I've done before, I'll look through my pile of photocopies and plans and books and I'll pull it out and look at it carefully. If I haven't done it before, I'll have to go into college early. An hour early if I'm really anxious. Twenty to thirty minutes early is usual. Then I photocopy, write role cards, do the pasting . . . all the tangible, physical stuff. If I really want it to go especially well, I note down the stages of the lesson on the back of my left hand. With this on my hand and the physical materials, I feel secure when I go in.

'I can't say that I "see", or visualise, the plan. It's more like I feel it. It's a sensual object. It's a shape that I feel. I need that framework. It's sort of internal.

'With the afternoon classes, I'm more likely to look for some *material* as a trigger. Something like a video and a set of worksheets. I have a sequence in my head (like pre-vocabulary teaching, pre-questions, watching the video, comprehension questions, discussion of the topic, etc.) and I'm just feeding that sequence or repertoire with bits of actual material. Where did I learn the sequences from? I don't know. Years of experience, I suppose. But probably observing teachers, too. Watching is the best way.

'I have a stock of pre-planned, ready-made lessons too. About a dozen. I know they work. But sometimes when I'm tempted to use one I think, "I *mustn't* do that one again. I'll bore everyone and myself silly!" So then I tend to go to the recipe books. They are very useful. You can dip in and pull out something you like.

'I think it's important to take something of yourself into the classroom too, like a favourite object, some flowers, a particular colour, so that students see you as a human being and so you can express a part of yourself. This self-expression releases a lot of the tension of being an "anonymous fount of wisdom". It's more creative and it lessens stress.'

Sara Shaw, an EFL teacher of 13 years' experience

Sara's solution to the planning problem is to find a starting point. It could be a piece of material, an idea she's used before or a nice activity in a teacher's resource book. Once she's found one idea, it usually triggers off a couple of other ideas and she's away.

FRAMEWORKS FOR 'BLOCK LESSONS'

Another way of tackling planning is to consider each lesson as a discrete block that can be filled with a particular *type* of lesson. For example, choosing from among the many types of lesson that exist, you could decide to do a 'Pre, In, Post' lesson on one of the receptive skills (i.e. reading or listening). This is a type of lesson you might choose to do if you believe that students' overall proficiency in the receptive skills will improve if they practise such presumed 'sub-skills' as 'reading for gist', 'noticing where sentences end' or 'listening for stressed words'.

Planning a Pre, In, Post lesson

1 Begin by choosing a sub-skill to work on.
2 Then choose appropriate material. So, if you decide to work on

reading for gist, you'll need to find a reading text of reasonable length (not too short) on one main topic and without too many distracting bits of detailed information.

3 Next, draw up a lesson plan containing one or more cycles of Pre, In and Post stages.

- **The 'Pre' Stage:** This stage should arouse students' interest and motivation and 'tune them into' the text, that is, introduce its topic, setting, cultural background and so on.
- **The 'In' Stage:** In this stage students work on concrete tasks designed to focus their attention on the target sub-skill. The tasks should be interesting and do-able so as to raise students' confidence.
- **The 'Post' Stage:** In this stage the tasks are checked. Additional tasks may be set to consolidate learning of language and subject matter.

4 Select tasks for each cycle. Let's suppose you have decided to work on reading for gist and have chosen a newspaper article on a forthcoming election. You could select the following tasks for two cycles.

First cycle:
'Pre' stage: Ask students if they read a newspaper. Ask too what sort of items they expect to be in a newspaper at the moment. Then ask students to read the text and come up with a two-word summary of what it's about.
'In' stage: The students read and prepare their summaries.
'Post' stage: Elicit and discuss the different summaries.

Second cycle:
'Pre' stage: Set a new task.
'In' stage: Students read the text and do the task.
'Post' stage: Students check their work on the task.

With this way of planning, you consider the lesson as a complete block. You choose an aim for the block, choose material that harmonises with the aim and then choose tasks that will enable you to pass through the three-stage cycle two or three times in the time available for the block.

As mentioned at the beginning of this section, there are many other models, or frameworks, that yield 'block' lessons. On a typical pre-service teacher training course trainees are often exposed to just a couple. One of these may well be the Presentation, Practice and Production (PPP) lesson framework. This is a type of lesson used especially when teaching a single or a small set of language items plus a communicative function/meaning of each item. Typical target items are: the Present Continuous (function: talking about future arrangements) and *What about -ing?* (function: introducing a suggestion).

However, this PPP lesson framework can equally well be used to teach a set of vocabulary (including phrases) or syntactical patterns such as '*it+be*+adjective+*to*+verb+complement' (as in *It's easy to think of an example*) or 'noun+noun' (as in *night job, student teacher . . .*). The basic stages of this type of lesson, also three in number, are:

1 **Presentation** The target item(s) are introduced so as to help students grasp meaning/communicative use as well as pronunciation and spelling.

2 **Practice** Students have repeated opportunities to say, and perhaps write, the new item(s). Activities in this stage are structured to ensure that students concentrate their attention on the new language (e.g. through repetition of a short dialogue featuring one or more target items). Later activities allow somewhat more freedom to transfer use of the target item(s) to other situations.

3 **Production** Students use the target items in real, or at least realistic, communication. For example, you may ask them to use a target item to say something true about themselves or about what they believe. Discussions and freer role plays are also typical activities at this stage.

So far, then, we've looked at these approaches to planning:

a using stock lessons with a genuinely different slant each time
b finding a starting point that then gives you an array of connected ideas
c using different *lesson frameworks*.

Each of these approaches means looking at lessons as 'blocks' or discrete units. A different approach is to think not so much in terms of 'vertical' connections within one lesson, but of 'horizontal' connections from lesson to lesson (see Fig. 2).

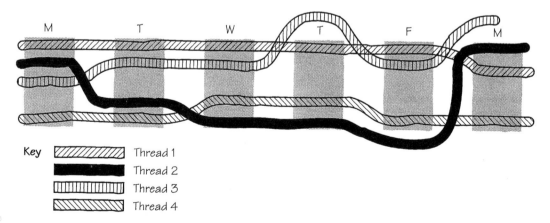

Key
- Thread 1
- Thread 2
- Thread 3
- Thread 4

Figure 2 'Horizontal' threads linking lesson to lesson

Here's another experienced teacher talking about his planning methods. This gives us a first taste of this fourth way of looking at lessons.

'When I get to school, I go up the back stairs and go straight to my classroom. That's my base at school. When I'm at home, I do my own reading of news-papers and *The New Scientist*, etc. with the students in mind – I do it with an awareness of them. I cut out things that I think will interest different students and I put their name on the top. Sometimes I'll put two names on top like "Akiko→Jean" if I think Akiko could pass her cutting on to Jean after she's read it. Some cuttings are so important I photocopy them for everyone.

'So, when I first arrive at school, I go to my base, the classroom. I have a little table in the corner. I take my wellies off or whatever. Then I rearrange the fur-niture, depending on the activity we're going to do. That way I take possession of the space. Then I put the clippings on their chairs. I'm very pleased with this "reading beginning". People come into class, take their coats off, finish the reading of their letters from home, then go on to the reading on their chairs. So nobody is ever really late. It's a *glide* into the lesson. An organic start. It's not sudden like in church when the celebrant enters! I like the edges of classtime to be fluid. So I'll finish five minutes early or I'll invade the coffee break and start the next lesson late, if I have the same class.

'The night before I will have planned something. But something will happen when I wake up. I'll think I could do something more interesting or do the same thing in a different way. I write a few lines down – about a quarter of a page with a mnemonic for the main stages. I keep all the plans and stick them together with tape [see Fig. 3]. I often don't look at the lesson plan at all in the classroom. But I need to know it's there. I need to know what the next stage is or I feel a bit panicky. I might also have on it the name of the person I want to work with in the break. I'll get them a coffee and we'll do some language correction or just chat.

Figure 3 Mario's stuck-together lesson plans

'With the main class I've got at the moment, I write them a group letter. I give a copy to everyone. They reply to me individually and then I write one letter back to the whole group, drawing on things they have written to me. Of course, I get their permission for this. And if it's too personal or if they ask me *not* to, of course I don't write in my group letter about what they've said.

'I would never go into a class with absolutely nothing in my head. Even if asked to substitute at the very last moment, I would still want to have a few things to propose. A menu choice. When I'm thinking of activities to do, I see and feel them in the *particular room* I'm going to be in – in that space. I think of exercises as "scenes" – *where* people meet and *how long* they stay there for, so . . . space and time, as well as what they do. I use space as the background. I also think of activities as "choreography" – as movement and rhythm and "togetherings". I feel quite happy about not using a plan that I've taken in. After all, you have bannisters up the side of the stairs but nobody says you have to hold onto them.

'With my main class at the moment, because it's an exam preparation class, there's a lot of reading and writing. They do loads of homework. So the preparation for the lesson, for me, is in the setting of the homework. For example, they have to retrieve eighteen words from a text and put them on cards (with definition, translation or collocation on the reverse) so that they can play a memory game with them in class. Or they have to buy a magazine they would not normally read and come ready to review it for others in the class. So, the teacher prepares the homework and in doing the homework the students prepare the class. What with this and the cuttings service and the letters, there's always plenty to do. We've done all manner of letter writing. Partly because, of all the skills in the FCE (*Cambridge First Certificate in English*) exam, letter writing, for this group, is going to be the most useful. They're all far away from home and living for letters anyway. And it's an interest of mine too – a drive for experimentation for me. So, it keeps me alive too.'

Mario Rinvolucri, who has about fifteen years' teaching experience spread over twenty years

Here is a teacher who doesn't think about each lesson as a block (e.g. 'Monday 9.00–10.50') but who tries to set up activities that run like threads through a series of lessons. For example, by setting up a newspaper-cutting service for the students, he has found a way of starting classes off and providing reading matter over quite a long series of lessons. **This is the type of planning and preparation work we want to look at in this book**. How can you set up a 'thread' that will run through a number of lessons fairly effortlessly instead of investing large amounts of time and energy before *each* lesson? But perhaps we should say more about what we mean by our term 'thread'.

1 What is a thread?

A thread is an activity or set of activities set up by you and your students. It can be used and reused although it doesn't have to be used *every* lesson. Once introduced in one lesson it can be picked up again quickly in later lessons with a minimum of explanation because it is familiar to everyone. Once a thread is set up, you have less to plan. Some threads you can use for just a minute of a lesson. Others can be used for twenty minutes or more. They can be used before or after other kinds of activities and with any kind of lesson type or shape. The same thread does not necessarily have to occur in the same part of every lesson; that depends on the thread.

2 An example thread

Let's take Mario's newspaper-cuttings service as an example of a thread. The basic idea is that you read through newspapers, journals and magazines with your students in mind. Every time you come across a headline, cartoon, article or letter that could interest or be relevant to a particular student or two, or to everyone, you cut it out. As students arrive in class they find a cutting waiting for them on their chairs and they set to and read it. They can use dictionaries, you or each other to help fathom out the meaning. That's the basic idea. Now let's look at whether this is a good thread or not.

3 What makes a 'good' thread?

The following are some of the criteria that we think make a good thread.

a The basic idea is negotiated with your students.

b It is enjoyable and useful to your students.

c It is used for as long as it remains enjoyable and useful and is dropped when interest in it wanes or the idea becomes over-routinised and dull.

d It deals with a particular aspect of teaching/learning a language and fosters a consistent, long-term approach to this aspect.

e It makes planning easier and faster, so creating a sense of ease in you, the teacher.

f It can be used from lesson to lesson with the minimum of effort, fuss and explanation time.

g It can be used from day to day at the same, or at different times, in the lesson.

h It includes slight variations in working process, so as to keep students guessing a little.

i It may build slowly from level to level, increasing in length and complexity.

j Individual students can use the idea to structure independent study.

k It can be adjusted to cater for individual differences.

An especially important criterion for a good thread is that it should build gradually from low-level to high-level language work. If the thread does this,

- you can start at the low level to give students confidence and then continue with the thread until the level begins to challenge them
- or, perhaps with a very confident group, you can start at the high-level end of the thread to see where the students' language is patchy.

You can, in either case, use the same thread, expecting different levels of work from different students in the same class.

4 Is the newspaper-cuttings service a good thread?

Let's see how the newspaper-cuttings service measures up against criteria (a)–(k) above.

a **Basic idea is negotiable:** Yes, it can be.

b **Enjoyable and useful:** Yes, apparently.

c **Can be dropped when interest in it wanes:** Yes, it could be.

d **Moves towards a long-term goal:** Yes. The class that this particular teacher had was preparing to take a British exam with a large, culturally-based reading comprehension component. Exposing the students to lots of authentic reading would seem to be a useful thing to do and something that can be tackled little by little over a period of time.

e **Makes planning easier and faster:** Probably not for every teacher, but for this particular teacher, who does a lot of reading in his private time, it is an enjoyable type of lesson preparation which he can combine with something he would do anyway.

f **Usable from lesson to lesson:** Yes. And once the idea has been set up, the students know what to do as soon as they spot the cuttings on their chairs.

g **Usable at the same, or different, times in the lesson:** Yes.

h **Includes variations in working process:** Yes. This thread allows for variations since a different task can be set each time. For example:
- Scan the piece quickly then tell your neighbour in one sentence what it's about.
- Pick out three words that belong to one lexical area.
- Read this thoroughly and prepare a comment incorporating your point of view.
- Read this carefully and teach your neighbour what you think is the most useful new word, phrase or idea you've learned.

i **Can build slowly from level to level, increasing in length and complexity:** Yes. It's just a matter of choosing appropriate texts.

j **Can help structure independent study:** Yes. The students can take over the idea by providing a cuttings service for each other, friends, or other classes or they can simply decide to keep up the habit of reading one piece of authentic English every day, no matter from what source.

k **Can cater for heterogeneity in the learning group:** Yes. You can give different people readings on different subjects, from different sources, and of different lengths and difficulty (e.g. the *Early Times* is easier than *The Financial Times*), and an easy headline is easier than a complex paragraph.

So, for this particular teacher and group of students, the cuttings service was a good thread.

5 What other types of thread are there?

THREAD TYPE 1: ACTIVITY FRAMEWORKS

Some activities and techniques can be used again and again from lesson to lesson with different content each time. A fairly standard example here is what some people call 'drilling' (also called 'controlled oral practice', 'chanting' or even 'oral standardisation'). Its components, from the teacher's point of view, include attracting attention, giving and highlighting a model sentence, conducting choral repetition, conducting individual repetition, reacting encouragingly and correcting errors. You can use the technique of drilling in any lesson wherever it's appropriate. The class will get used to your particular gestures and such teacher talk as, 'Listen everybody!', 'Now you', 'Again' and so on. They will know what's expected and will react accordingly (if they feel like it!).

What we are talking about here is an activity or technique *framework*. Again, once a group of students has met the framework in one guise, you can use it again and again with different content and generally be able to do so with very little time spent on preliminary explanation.

There are many examples of such frameworks besides drilling. Here's another one:

'Name Scrabble' is a simple name-learning activity where students gradually build up an arrangement of their names (e.g. on a poster) by interlocking them as in a Scrabble game (see Fig. 4).

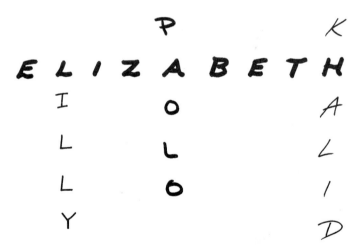

Figure 4 'Name Scrabble' – a first incarnation of the Scrabble framework

One way of reusing the 'Name Scrabble' framework is to ask students, in pairs, to write down in Scrabble form, in their notebooks, all the target language words they know for colours. Thus, two students might produce the arrangement shown in Figure 5.

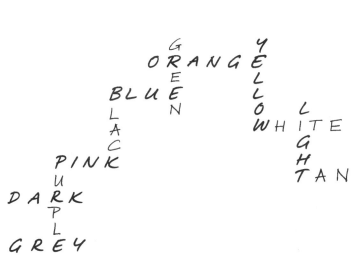

Figure 5 'Vocabulary Scrabble' – a second incarnation of the Scrabble framework

CAN THE SCRABBLE FRAMEWORK MAKE A GOOD THREAD?

a Basic idea is negotiable: Yes. After its initial use (when students learn how it works), you can all discuss whether and when to use it again for different purposes.

b Enjoyable and useful: Yes, potentially.

c Can be dropped when interest in it wanes: Yes.

d Moves towards a long-term goal: Yes. The Scrabble framework can be used again and again for reviewing or teaching vocabulary in other topic areas (e.g. sports, vegetables, emotions) or for different word classes (e.g. verbs). Additionally, students learn a *process* which they can apply in their own study (see (j) below).

e Makes planning easier and faster: Yes. Once you and your students know the framework and have identified a topic area to work within, the rest is easy.

f Usable from lesson to lesson: Provided the language, subject matter and the arrangement of people (i.e. all at the board, sitting in groups, etc.) are varied, it is reusable, albeit not so regularly as the newspaper-cuttings service.

g Usable at the same, or different, times in the lesson: Yes.

h Includes variations in working process: Yes. For example, you can use it in different arrangements of people (e.g. the whole class taking turns at the board, pairs sitting . . .).

i Can build slowly from level to level, increasing in length and complexity: Yes, but just how and to what extent depends on the 'rules' you adopt. For example, the following version, 'Association Scrabble', is suitable for an intermediate/advanced class that has just read a text or set of texts.

Association Scrabble:

1 One by one, students write up on the board in a Scrabble arrangement an item of vocabulary they remember from the text(s). Or, if they prefer, they can write up a word or phrase which they associate with a word or phrase from the text(s), if that word has already been written up on the board by another student. Thus, if the text contains the word *slink* a student can either write that word on the board or (if it is already on the board) an association such as *panther* (see Fig. 6 for an example). (Vocabulary from the text and associations can be written in different colours.)

2 After a set time, or after a previously stipulated number of words has been written up, ask students to explain the associations. For example, 'I wrote *panther* because of *slink*. Slinking is how panthers walk'.

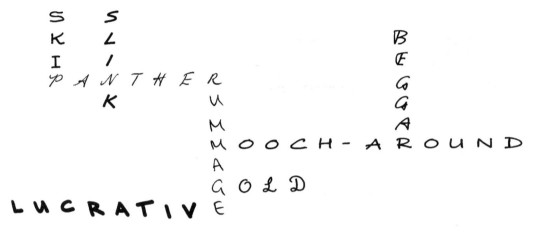

Figure 6 'Association Scrabble' – a third incarnation. This shows part of an arrangement created in an advanced class that had read a set of texts written by English people about their impressions of New York City

j **Can help structure independent study:** Yes. For example, either individually, or in pairs or groups, students could build Scrabble arrangements to check their recollection of recently encountered vocabulary.

k **Can cater for heterogeneity in the learning group:** Yes. Each student has considerable choice in what to add to the arrangement.

THE REUSABILITY OF ACTIVITY FRAMEWORKS

Almost any activity has a framework that can be used again and again with different content. The content in one lesson where the framework is used need not relate to the content of another lesson were the framework is used, just as the Scrabble framework can be applied to names, colour words or vocabulary from a text, in fact, to any set of vocabulary you or your class decide to consolidate and extend. Many other activity frameworks can be used for different purposes and with different content in different lessons. For example, almost any of the various ways of doing dictation (e.g. teacher to students at slow speed with no questions from students, teacher to students at natural speed with questions allowed from students, or student to student in pairs), dialogue building (e.g. starting with a picture, with key words, or with a story) or picture composition (e.g. you display a numbered sequence of pictures and elicit an oral story from the class, or students order a jumbled set of pictures and write a story). Arrangements and movements of people, e.g. students in pairs or students in small groups moving from table to table, can also be considered as a type of thread since these choreographical elements can recur and evolve from lesson to lesson.

THREAD TYPE 2: LESSON BANDS

Some general categories of activity can be used over a series of lessons. For example:

- warm-ups
- one-minute breaks/pauses
- fillers
- review
- pronunciation work
- returning and setting homework.

These general categories include activities that are otherwise unrelated to each other. Let's take one of these categories as an example: 'warm-ups'.

You might decide for a 9.00 a.m. class that you'll begin each lesson with a five-minute warm-up time devoted to getting students thinking and working together. Thanks to the many teachers' resource, or

9 a.m.	Mon	Tues	Wed	Thurs	Fri
	Warm-ups and getting-to-know-you activities				
10					
	One minute break activities				
11					
	BREAK TIME		BREAK TIME		
	What did you learn last lesson?				
	Fun filler exercises	Fun filler exercises	Fun filler exercises		
1 p.m.	LUNCH LUNCH	LUNCH LUNCH	LUNCH LUNCH	LUNCH	
	Grammar practice games				
	Getting organised for homework				

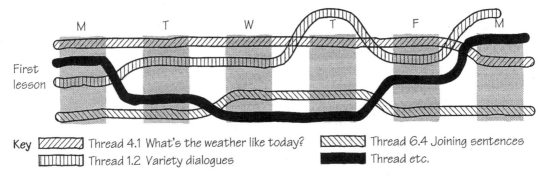

First
lesson

Key
Thread 4.1 *What's the weather like today?*   Thread 6.4 *Joining sentences*
Thread 1.2 *Variety dialogues*   Thread etc.

Figure 8 A timetable with bands and the threads of a band

'recipe' books around these days, you have access to a wide variety of possible activities (or threads) to fill the band of warm-up slots that now stretches across your weekly timetables. Indeed, you could make a number of 'lesson bands' (as in Fig. 8) with the help of different teachers' resource books.

The parts of lessons *not* using bands could be devoted to the use of coursebooks and/or to blocks of work structured according to the Pre, In, Post model, the PPP model or some other model of lesson structure, e.g. Counselling Learning, Total Physical Response, or Task-based Learning.

From lesson to lesson

The separate sections of this book (1.1, 1.2, etc.) each have a sub-section headed *From lesson to lesson*. This is where you will find out how to use the activity as a thread by developing it and extending its scope over a series of lessons.

Summary

We have mentioned in this introduction two types of lesson threads that teachers often use. These are *Activity frameworks* and *Lesson bands*. Teachers thus already think of running ideas from lesson to lesson. However, since much TESOL training can, through pressure of time, force teachers to concentrate on one lesson at a time (the *next* lesson!), one block at a time, we would like in this book to redress that imbalance by encouraging planning across a *series* of lessons through the use of threads. Each of the chapter titles in Part 1 is the name of a lesson band. Within each chapter are a number of threads for the band.

The first part of this book is therefore devoted to helping you build up a repertoire of **threads**. That is, ideas which:

- once set up, can run from lesson to lesson, or skip from alternate lesson to alternate lesson without involving too much planning time

- build slowly, from elementary to advanced, thus allowing you to jump in and start using them at a level suitable to *your* class, or to use them with multi-level classes
- go beyond the one-off recipe, to work that progresses and builds from lesson to lesson
- provide a blend of familiarity and novelty
- students find interesting and may continue on their own
- you can pick up and drop whenever you feel it's appropriate
- you can blend into your own normal style of teaching and planning. Even if you must conform to a rigid syllabus, you can use most of these threads to increase the amount of review, consolidation and extension of syllabus elements
- are ideas you can use *today*!

Part 2 is slightly different. It is about what teachers can learn. It is still about lesson planning but it deals with the part of a lesson plan headed 'teacher development' or 'what I want to learn/experiment within this lesson'. It is still about threads but this time they are threads of classroom practice that can prevent teacher burn out.

Tessa Woodward
Seth Lindstromberg
Ickham, Kent
1994

PART 1

Student themes: building from lesson to lesson

INTRODUCTION

In Part 1 we look at how to develop interesting ways of evolving work in areas which are important to your students, e.g. building vocabulary or increasing fluency. Our basic aims are to explain how to:

- create sequences of lessons which give learners a feeling of progress and of a *relationship* between lessons
- plan more efficiently by taking the emphasis off planning individual lessons and placing it on building consolidation and extension activities into lesson sequences right from the start.

CHAPTER 1

The beginnings of fluency and beyond

Many coursebooks and teacher trainers exhort teachers to do lots of pair- and groupwork with their classes. Teachers who try it, especially with monolingual groups, will sometimes discover to their dismay that pair- and groupwork immediately causes most students to break into their mother tongue. This is probably not due to bad class management on the part of the teacher but to a number of other factors, namely:

i   It's more natural to speak to someone of your own mother tongue in that language rather than in another one.
ii Your mother tongue is the language that is most *real* to you, so whenever you do anything that feels real (rather than simulated), you'll tend to use it.
iii Pair- and groupwork involve communicative operations such as: discovering who you are working with, greeting them, clarifying what's to be done, commenting on it, deciding who is to start, deciding whether the task has been done properly, whether it is over or not, and so on. These operations may presuppose a very subtle use of language. Students who lapse into their mother tongue may do so because they simply do not know how to carry out these oral tasks in English.

We have, then, to be aware of two areas of language:

● Any language items that are the object of study and which occur in the texts and exercises that the students do
● the 'interaction language' that students need in order to do the tasks you set and to deal with each other and with you in the ways outlined above in (**iii**).

This chapter begins by showing ways of working on this second area of language. We look at ways of making short, planned dialogues an ongoing feature of classroom interaction. Thus, this lesson band is called 'The beginnings of fluency and beyond'. Except for one sub-activity, you need nothing but a board. In class, the dialogues take very little time to set up; indeed, briskness and brevity are essential for best results.

The main out-of-class work consists in working out what classroom situations your students will need to use natural English in. Secondly, you need to consider a range of things they could say in these situations. An hour or so of brainstorming with a colleague should generate (a) an ample list of headings such as 'deciding who in a pair/group is going to start first or take which role' and (b) under each heading, a list of expressions – such as gambits (e.g. *Me first?*) and replies (e.g. *Yes, it's your turn*) – which you want your students to learn (see Fig. 9 for examples of such lists). If you have access to native speakers, a good way of making sure these gambits, replies, etc. are truly natural is to eavesdrop while native speakers are, for example, starting pairwork. There may well be a difference between the phrases you think will be used in this setting and the phrases which actually are used.

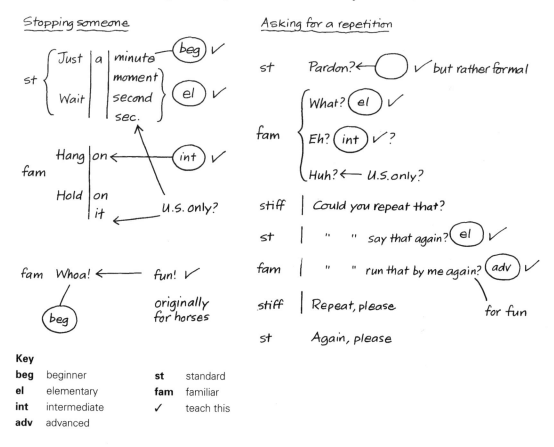

Key

beg	beginner	**st**	standard
el	elementary	**fam**	familiar
int	intermediate	✓	teach this
adv	advanced		

Figure 9 Fragment of teacher's notes made after brainstorming teachable interaction language

1.1

LEVEL
Beginner–
Intermediate

TIME
A few minutes+

MATERIALS
None

FOCUS

For students
Learning and
practising
interaction
language; initially,
developing the
ability to respond
quickly to gambits
in the target
language;
eventually,
initiating
conversations;
improving
intonation

For you
Breaking down
the target
language silence
between you and
your students

ECHO DIALOGUES

Echo dialogues can be a stepping stone to Thread 1.2, *Variety dialogues*. Its gist is that in every lesson, at some or at various points, you very briefly and briskly introduce/review, and use, a short realistic exchange which students need when working in English with you or with a partner/group. The idea can really come in handy in those awkward, cool classes that respond sluggishly or not at all when you ask them questions and which bring you to wonder, 'Did I say anything? Am I here? What's going on?' The secret to the idea's success is that students don't have to think much in order to answer. Besides repeating what they hear, all they have to do is alter the intonation. To initiate, all they need to do is remember a single word or a short phrase. Thus, this is repetition with a communicative purpose. It's the easiest possible way to begin dialogue work. Even so, a surprising amount of extremely useful language can be learned.

Introducing the thread (*at beginner/elementary level*)

1 On the board, draw two arrows. Perhaps add two quickly sketched faces, like this:

Figure 10

2 Take an expression that you think your students know the meaning of, *OK*, for instance. Point to the arrow on the left and say 'OK?' (i.e. with rising intonation). Signal your class to repeat. Point to the other arrow and say 'OK' with falling intonation. Signal your class to repeat.

3 Lead practice. Pointing to the first arrow, say 'OK?' Point to the other arrow and signal the class to speak. They should say 'OK' with falling intonation.

4 Then do the dialogue with a single student. If intonation is too flat, sweep an arm up or down to indicate a bigger pitch range and signal the student to try again.

5 Signal two students (on opposite sides or corners of the class) to do the dialogue.

6 Quickly form pairs. Signal students to do the dialogue once, swap partners, then do it again.

Here are just a few of the many more words and phrases that make useful echo dialogues in beginner and low elementary classes:

One word: *Yes, No, Right, Ready, Start, Stop, OK, Alright, Finished, Now, Enough, Break, Coffee, Tea, Again, Understand, Next, Open, Shut, Louder, Slower, Faster, Better, Easy, Swap, Here/Present, Ill, Everything, Right, Wrong, Capital, Comma, Paragraph, Pairs, Groups, Today, Tomorrow*

Two words: *Once more, Too fast/slow, Got/Get it, Next one, Not yet, Clean/Erase it, Go/Move on, Switch on/off, Spell it, This/that one, Had enough, Start again, Sentence/Question/Page one*

Three words: *Do/Play/Say/Read it again, From the beginning, To the end, Turn it over, Rub it out, Clean it off*

From lesson to lesson

→ Integrate these exchanges into classroom routine. For example, if you've written something on the board which students are copying, make as if to begin cleaning it off. Say 'Finished?' Signal for a response, perhaps by pointing at a downward curving arrow you've left on display somewhere, or perhaps by making a downward sweep of an arm. If you see that someone is still copying the board work, you can teach them how to say, 'No! *Not* finished!' When they say it, walk away from the board and leave the writing up for a while. In this way show students that they can use these simple phrases to accomplish something.

→ Introduce more and more departures from pure repetition, but stick to the pattern of short, single-exchange, question-and-answer dialogues, for example:

A: Difficult homework?
B: Very difficult! / No, easy

→ Introduce simple extensions like: '(Do you) want to be A?'/'No, B.' This is for partners deciding who's going to play person A and who person B.

→ Follow on with substitutions that depend on point of view: *I* for *you*, *here* for *there*, *this* for *that* and so on. For example:

A: My turn?
B: Your turn.
A: Finished?
B: Yes, I'm finished.
A: Coffee?
B: Yes! And you?

RATIONALE

No matter how heterogeneous your class, *Echo dialogues* practically guarantees that over a number of lessons *everybody* can achieve a minimum level of oral fluency. Challenge your more proficient students by encouraging them to embellish the expressions taught.

1.2

LEVEL
Elementary+

TIME
A few minutes+

MATERIALS
Blank cards
needed for one
sub-activity

FOCUS
For students
Participating in
common
conversational
exchanges
spontaneously
and with good
linguistic
accuracy; taking
on new ways of
saying things one
can already say;
comprehensive
review of versatile
conversational
gambits and
replies or reply
strategies; using
English in class-
room interaction,
beginning with
grammatically
simple colloquial
'clipped' forms;
language needed
to get more
information out of
you

For you
Gradually
converting the
working language
of the classroom
to English

VARIETY DIALOGUES

Variety dialogues continues the *Echo dialogues* thread (1.1) of especially common and useful conversational gambits and replies. At
lower levels, it may involve teaching expressions before they, or even
their speech functions, occur in your syllabus or coursebook. You
will be moving your students ahead more quickly in certain areas.
Later on, within these areas, you will be relying on your coursebook more for review exercises than for ideas for presentation and
practice.

As with *Echo dialogues*, the motto is 'grammarless beginnings'. That
is, the aim is to enable students to participate as early as possible in
real conversations without having to worry about things like auxiliary
verbs. 'Grammarless' phrases are often just what native speakers
would say anyway. Put differently, lower-level learners are started out
not on a diet of difficult full forms like *Have you got any spare paper?*,
but on simpler 'clipped' forms whenever they exist in everyday
English. This thread of 'grammarless' beginnings means beginning
with the most 'clipped' form and then adding words from lesson to
lesson or from level to level according to students' ability. Here are
some examples:

Function: requesting/borrowing something

Spare paper? (pointing to the other's notepad)→Any spare paper?→Got any
spare paper?→You got any spare paper?→Have you got any spare paper?

Function: Parting at the end of a meeting/class

Bye. Nice weekend!→Bye! Have a nice weekend!→Bye! Hope you have a nice
weekend!
(Meeting again after a weekend)
Nice weekend?→Have a nice weekend?→Did you have a nice weekend?

Teachers and coursebooks often start with relatively hard full
forms. This places an immense hurdle in the way of participation in
everyday talk. What's more, it seems that many teachers and coursebook writers never do get around to devoting much (if any) attention
to clipped forms. Thus, *Variety dialogues* has applications even in
intermediate and advanced classes.

Finally:

- It is important to be clear that the language you teach within this
  framework is *not* to be taught all at once. Far from it. *Variety dialogues* involves *step-by-step* extension of students' repertoires of
  expressions over a number (possibly dozens or scores) of lessons.
  In a heterogeneous class, the less proficient students can stick to
  the original clipped form for a particular function (e.g. *Spare X?* for
  borrowing), while more proficient students can be encouraged to
  use a variety of forms, including complete ones.

- It is vital to regularly conduct short bursts of review/use of one or two of the communicative areas that have already been covered.
- When reviewing a given function (e.g. greeting), insist that more proficient students use a wide selection from among the expressions they have learned so far. However, do take time to clarify, as new wordings are introduced, how they differ in register.

Preparation

1 Decide on an area of communication:
   - which your students are weak in or in which, at least, there is room for improvement or broadening of repertoire and
   - which should figure in natural interaction among people who work in a group from time to time.

   Thus, in a twice-weekly class of beginners, you might decide on 'greeting someone you know but haven't seen for a day or two'.

2 Think of a simple exchange for your chosen speech function, for example,

A: Hello. How are you?
B: Fine, thanks. And you?
A: Fine.

Introducing the thread (at beginner/elementary level)

1 Introduce and practise your dialogue in your normal way. In the case of a greeting dialogue, the beginning of class is obviously the best time for this. It's a short dialogue, so five minutes' work each day should be plenty.

2 Finish by asking students to write the dialogue in their notebooks at the top of a new page (perhaps in the back of their books) under a heading they can understand, such as, 'Hello', 'Meeting again' or 'Greet and reply' (depending on their level and/or whether or not you can explain vocabulary in the heading in your students' mother tongue). Ask them to leave the rest of that page blank.

From lesson to lesson

→ At the start of subsequent lessons, get students to greet you or respond to your greetings in the way learned. Get them to run through this dialogue with each other quickly in pairs, too.

→ When you've seen that your class has taken this on board, teach a variation for each line of the dialogue, e.g.:

A: Hello. How are you?→Hi. How are you?
B: Fine.→OK. And you?→How about you?
A: Fine.→Not too bad.

→ Have students do the earlier version with the person on their left and the new version with the person on their right. Finish by asking students to find the earlier dialogue in their notebooks and then write the variation next to or under it.

→ Make a point of continuing to have a minute (or less) of greeting dialogues at the beginning of the next few sessions.

→ After another couple of sessions (or sooner if students have learned quickly), begin to introduce one or two variations for each line, e.g.:

A: Good morning!→Morning!
How's it going?→How are you doing?→How're things?
B: Pretty good.→So so. What about you?, etc.

Encourage students to use the full range of expressions they have learned as follows:

● After a bout of greeting, ask them to tick the expressions (in their notebooks) that they used.
● Before each new bit of dialogue practice, ask them to review by looking in their notebooks.
● Then, in the dialogue practice, they use expressions with no ticks or with few ticks by them.

→ If there is space, students go around the room and do a different version of the dialogue (though following the same dialogue structure) with each student they meet.

→ At the beginning of subsequent (though not necessarily all) classes, encourage students to have brief, natural greeting dialogues. Continue to feed in new expressions from time to time.

→ Next, introduce another basic dialogue for a common speech function, for example, 'saying goodbye at the end of a meeting/class', 'asking to borrow something', 'asking someone for clarification', 'apologising for being late to a class/meeting' and so on, e.g.:

Apologising:
A: Sorry.
B: That's OK.

Once this has been learned, add alternatives within the same structure as before:

A: Sorry I'm late.
B: That's OK.

Then:

A: Sorry I'm late. I had a problem with . . .
        It was the . . .
B: Oh, I see . . . / Oh. What a shame!

→ If you have to check attendance in a large class, teach and encourage students to use alternatives to *Yes* and *Present*. Introduce as much brisk variety as possible, for example,

Teacher: Hiroshi. OK?
Hiroshi: OK.
Teacher: Jean. Busy weekend?
Jean: Mmm.
Teacher: José. How're things?
Jose: Not bad.
Teacher: Helen. Present?
Helen: Present.

→   *Advanced level:* These students are, by definition, good at coming out with full forms. Often, though, they use almost no clipped forms. As a result they may sound pompous and verbose in everyday chat. Unlike with beginners, teaching meanings should seldom be necessary. Just sketch a situation and elicit the full forms that your students have already learned for the speech functions involved.

→   Tell advanced learners to chop off everything that's easy to infer or take for granted. For example, for the situation 'in class, before a coffee break', you might elicit:

A: Would you like a coffee?
B: Yes, I would like one. (in Step 1 in 'Introducing the thread' above)

More natural clipped forms include *Like a coffee?/Yes, I would.* After prompting, you might even elicit:

A: Coffee?
B: Mmm!

Although you might have to teach this!

→   As you will not be building up to longer expressions at this level, the variety of new expressions for some communicative areas may not be great. Thus, you will be able to cover more areas in fewer lessons than would be the case with a lower-level class. On different days review different communicative areas. Exchanges and variations can be practised in a minute or two per communicative area.

→   Use this activity, called 'Slip It In'.

Materials: Slips of paper or card, each with a snippet of interaction language or an excerpt from a variety dialogue on it, e.g. *How about you?, What does . . . mean?, You start, Busy weekend?* Or, at a higher level, ones like, *I've got something to add about that,* etc.

1 Students each get one card. They keep them confidential.
2 Students try to slip what's on their card into the stream of talk during whole-class work sometime before the end of the lesson. Whenever a student manages to use their snippet so naturally that no one notices, the student turns the card over. The aim is for

everyone to turn their cards over in this way. You can use quiet times to walk round and check on who said what.

Variations: Various scoring systems are possible, including, e.g. extra points for successfully spotting when someone else has just said her/his bit of 'planted' language, loss of points for guessing this wrong, division of the class into teams and giving out more than one card to each student.

COMMENTS

Variety dialogues brings variety in your classes in another sense besides that of students learning a lot of different expressions. There is variety in whether they choose to use full or part forms. There is also variety in the communicative areas you work in. Some lessons you begin by having students review their greeting dialogues. Other times you get straight on with your lesson, but then later ask your students to use different ways of asking for clarification of what someone has just said. So, the thread that runs throughout 1.1 and 1.2 is building genuine interaction in the classroom between students, and between students and you, *in English.*

1.3

LEVEL
Lower elementary
– Upper
intermediate

TIME
2 minutes

MATERIALS
None

FOCUS
Improving
students' ability
to recognise and
produce common,
phonetically
compacted
phrases

BIRDSONG

Preparation

Choose a commonly recurring stretch of two or more words that your students tend to say in a stilted, robotic fashion. Let's take *does he do* as an example. This they might generally say with equal stress on each word and full pronunciation of the *does* and the /h/. (Generally, good bits of language to work with will consist mostly or completely of articles, pronouns, auxiliaries, prepositions and basic main verbs like *do, be, have* and *like.*)

The first time you do this, don't tell your students what you have in mind!

Introducing the thread (*at lower elementary level*)

1 Tell them you're all going to practise an English birdsong, namely, 'duzzydoo'. Say it in a musical, cuckoo-like way. Get students to mimic you. Get them to tap out its rhythm.
2 Ask everyone to whisper it to themselves several times quickly.
3 Right around the class, everyone says it once as quickly as possible after the person before.
4 Now, ask if anyone can use 'duzzydoo' in a sentence. Someone might say, 'We have no bird in our country who says "duzzydoo".' But you're after different game. If no one has realised they've been practising *does he do*, give a model sentence yourself, *Does he do his homework everyday?*

5 Try to elicit another sentence containing your chosen phrase. Ask students to repeat it a few times, perhaps very quietly, to themselves. Encourage the birdsong pronunciation. As soon as you stop this activity, students will, of course, backslide horribly into their old robotic ways. But in the long run, you will succeed with some learners and even with the others their ability to recognise these phrases when they hear them in the mouths of fluent speakers is bound to improve.

VARIATIONS

You don't, of course, need to present your phrases as birdsongs. Instead, present them as strange names or as noises. For example, get students to mimic the sound of a train by rapidly chanting, 'aiwannagetoff, aiwannagetoff . . .'/*I want to get off*. (In this variation the message of the words can have a topical link with the sound imitated.)

From lesson to lesson

→ Review previous 'birdsongs'. ('What was that birdsong we did the other day? The one that José did so perfectly?')

→ Introduce new ones, for example, 'dushydoo'/*does she do*, 'dishydoo'/*did she do*, 'diddydoo'/*did he do*, 'whenzit'/*when is it*, 'wujal  kta' *would you like to*, 'wudentuv'/*wouldn't have*.

NOTE

If you decide to write the phrases phonemically (which isn't absolutely necessary), your two options are to do so in an *ad hoc* fashion, as we have done here, or to use the International Phonemic Alphabet. If your students don't know the IPA, try teaching it. After all, British learners' dictionaries use the IPA in their pronunciation guides.

→ Combine birdsongs in two-person dialogues. Begin with just the 'birdsong' parts and see if anyone can think of completions. If you write the dialogues on the board, indicate stress and intonation somehow. For example:

A. 'wujadoomeeah' favour?   **B.** 'ahwilif  ' can.

or

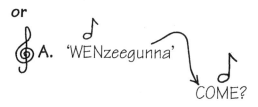

A. 'WENzeegunna'   COME?

B. He 'SEDDeedkummet'   FOUR.

→ Tell 'Knock, knock' jokes that play on how a name (or a word that could be a name in some part of the world) can sound like (part of) an English phrase spoken at fast natural speed. For example:

A Knock, knock.
B Who's there?
A William.
B William, who?
A Will you make me a sandwich, I'm hungry.

Other examples are: 'Hans'/'Hands up, your money or your life'; 'Scot'/'Scot nothing to do with you'; 'Michael'/'*Mike*'ll be here later, let *me* in now'; 'Faiwa'/'If I were you, I'd call the police, I'm a burglar'; 'Wudin'/'Wouldn't it be nice to give me a cup of tea?'; 'Jamaica'/'Your wife, could you make her stop singing, it's driving me crazy'; 'Duzzy'/'My friend Bill, does he still live here?'.

ACKNOWLEDGEMENT
Tessa learnt 'dishygo, diddygo' drills from Dilys Brown in the seventies.

COINS

Introducing the thread

1 Ask every student to hold one to four coins or other small, hard objects in one hand. The more students in your class, the fewer the coins; more coins for a hard text than for an easy one. Adults will usually have enough coins, but have a stock of coins, buttons or pebbles in reserve.

2 Tell them that you're going to read a text out loud to them (or tell a story from memory). The job of each student is to interrupt you once if they start with one coin, twice if they start with two and so on. They signal each interruption by plonking down a coin. When they interrupt, they can ask you to clarify something you've just said, or they can ask you something *totally unconnected* with what you're reading out. It's up to them.

Either show them the text you're going to read or tell them about how long the reading or telling will take. Then explain to them that if they use up their coins too soon, they might not be able to ask a question about something near the end which they genuinely don't understand. Add that if, on the other hand, they get stuck with coins when you've finished, their ignominy will be made public to the whole class!

If you think it necessary, write up on the board a few starters such as:

Uhh . . .
What does . . . mean?
What was the bit before/after . . .?
Could you elaborate a bit on . . .?

● In mixed-ability classes, less proficient students can have these gambits written out in full on paper beside them, medium-level students can have some single words as an *aide-mémoire*, whereas the most proficient students can be asked to use the gambits from memory.

3 Begin telling your story or reading out loud.

VARIATION

At elementary level: Hand out copies of the text so that students can follow along as you read. Omit the occasional word as you read. Students thump their tables (or clap) when they notice an omission and call out:

You	missed (out)		after	X.
	left out	the word	before	
	skipped		between X and Y.	

And/Or occasionally say a different word than is in the text. Students call out:

1.4

LEVEL
Elementary+

TIME
10–30 minutes

MATERIALS
Three or four small objects per student; one longish, moderately challenging text for you to read out loud or a story to tell from memory

FOCUS
Review/extension of students' stock of phrases for asking a speaker to clarify; listening; practising basic discussion skills such as interrupting, dealing with interruptions and so on; possibly, reading out loud (for the speaker)

Didn't you say X instead of Y?
You said X instead of Y.

From lesson to lesson

→ Add more interrupting phrases.
→ Bring in stranger and stranger objects.
→ Use texts containing material you wish to review.
→ Apply the technique to short lectures.
→ Students take the role of speaker. One student can read a whole text, or students can take turns reading paragraphs. (Give readers the text to read before the lesson and spend a bit of time with them, helping them rehearse their reading.)
→ Dispense with the coins. If you want a talk by you or someone else to be punctuated with interventions from the class, just say, 'Lots of questions, please. Like when you used the coins.'

RATIONALE

- This is a very effective ploy for getting usually taciturn students to react to extended talk. To ration extra-voluble students to their fair share of talking time, strictly enforce the rule 'no more objects, no more interruptions'.
- *Coins* is good for teaching and practising interruption language and questioning in general.
- In the variation where a student reads out loud, motivation is raised owing to the fact that speakers do not feel they're speaking into a vacuum.
- The rationale for allowing students to ask questions about *anything* is as follows: anyone who doesn't have three (or four) genuine questions about what they hear – instead of feeling forced to ask fake or frivolous questions about something they already understand – can ask *genuine* questions about something else. On a recent course, these wider questions touched on, for example, the social programme, the due date of a long writing assignment and whether we could rejig the timetable to allow the class to go to the Wednesday market.

ACKNOWLEDGEMENT
We were reminded of the variation by Steve Roberts.

CHAPTER 2

Silence and sounds

The listening threads in this lesson band can be done with commercial or off-air recordings (if this is legal in your country) or live voices. They can be based on scripted, semi-scripted or unscripted utterances and texts (as with Threads 2.3–2.8), or on music and other non-verbal sounds, as with *Background music* (2.1) and *Silence and sounds* (2.2).

Threads 2.3–2.8 describe specific listening tasks. One way of using these tasks is to have a few goes with one before introducing the next. Another way of proceeding, suitable for mixed-ability classes, is to use different tasks at the same time but with different students. For example, *Which words did you hear?* (2.6) could be suitable for lower proficiency students in a class. Threads 2.3–2.8 all build towards *Catching English from the air* (2.8), which equips students with a method of learning from any authentic listening they are exposed to.

BACKGROUND MUSIC

Introducing the thread

1 Before the beginning of each class turn on some music you like. Instrumental music generally works best; it should definitely not be raucous. Keep the volume low: the music should be there, but barely there. Tessa likes it as background music for herself, as she settles into the room, does her preliminary board work and so on.
2 Keep the music on as students drift in. You can leave the music on until the tape runs out. (Often, someone will ask if they can turn it over.) Or, turn it off when you begin the class or when your warm-up activity is finished. If anyone asks if you can turn off the music, take a vote. Also let people switch places so that those who like it are near the music, those who dislike it sit away from it.

2.1

LEVEL
Any

TIME
Variable

MATERIALS
A music cassette and a cassette recorder

FOCUS
Relaxing yourself and others; possibly providing a talking point

From lesson to lesson

→ Use different music each time, perhaps varying the country of origin.

→ Play background music especially during pair- and groupwork.

→ After five or six times of playing background music, don't bring any in. Generally someone will ask, 'Where's the music?' If so, invite them, or someone else, to bring in a cassette for the next lesson, and the lesson after that, and so on. (If you don't want 'noisy' music, say so!)

If no one asks why there's no music, perhaps it's a good idea to drop playing music in that class, or only bring some in, for yourself, if and when you especially feel like it.

RATIONALE

● Music can act as a conversation stimulus. It can generate, or provide the opportunity to teach language like: *Turn it down, Can I move?, Let's swap places, What's that?, What kind of music is that?, What instrument is that?, Is that (Japanese) music?.*

● Many people find background music relaxing.

● It can be a terrific help in getting pair- and groupwork off to a good start since it provides a level of background noise that seems to make it easier for people to start talking.

● Using different kinds of stimulus in class draws out different students. For example, the very musical student might not be among the most forthcoming in the class, but this could change with a bit of music in the air.

● Carefully selected music can focus and stimulate students' imaginations in ways that link well with particular activities and topics. (See especially Cranmer and Laroy 1992.)

SILENCE AND SOUNDS

The basic activity is especially useful if done before a discussion or before any listening involving a recorded text in order to quieten a class down and to help them to concentrate.

Introducing the thread (at beginner level)

1 Tell your students that in a minute you're going to ask them to close their eyes and not say anything. Tell them they'll hear four or five sounds and each time they hear one they have to think of the name in English of the object making the sound. Give them an example. Thus you might say to them: 'You hear "vrrrrmmm" [noise of car passing]. You think "car". But in the next examples, don't say the word like I did, just *think* it, and try to remember the English word.'
2 Proceed with the activity. Begin with sounds that are clearly associated with particular objects (e.g. feet walking, coins jingling, door opening, paper tearing, zipper moving, board pen squeaking), and leave some thinking time between each sound.
3 After you've made all the sounds, ask students to open their eyes and tell a neighbour the nouns. Afterwards, check to make sure they're right.

From lesson to lesson

→ Add new sounds; review old ones.
→ After doing this thread for a while with beginner or elementary students, begin to introduce verb phrases (*not* full sentences) either for earlier sounds or for new ones, for example: to *car* add *going past*, to *door* add *opening/someone opening a door*.
→ An alternative, at intermediate level, is to introduce a series of typically associated noises, perhaps ones that suggest a story. For example: Footsteps approach, door opening, voice says 'Oh! Sorry!', door closes quickly, footsteps walk away, voice says 'Hmmmm' in a tone suggesting there might be something to gossip about.
   First elicit nouns and verbs. In pairs, students then tell a story suggested by the sounds.
→ Move on to longer sound sequences. Divide each one over a few lessons, each time reviewing what's been heard before. You can make the sounds on the spot or pre-record them at home. If you don't want to make the sounds yourself, two books by Maley and Duff (1975 and 1978) are accompanied by cassettes of usable sounds and sound sequences.
→ Focus on particular topics, for example, sounds associated with a particular job (e.g. carpentry), or sport (e.g. fishing), or place (e.g. kitchen, street, garage).
→ Pairs or groups of students make their own tapes of sounds for

2.2

LEVEL
Any

TIME
5 minutes+; extensions can last an hour or more

MATERIALS
Optional props for sound effects; cassette recorder; blank/published cassettes

FOCUS
Building vocabulary, especially that connected with the topic of 'sound'; enhancing recall by building networks of associations; varying the type of stimulus from visual to auditory

presentation to others. Or students can make their sound effects live while others listen with eyes closed. Be prepared for a bit of rudeness!

→ With more proficient students, teach imitative noises and customary ways of trying to represent the sound in writing or speech such as when one is trying to describe physical events in an especially vivid fashion. For example, 'I leaned over the stew and "kerplop", in fell my glasses!' The chart below gives some examples of verbs and other words in English which are used to represent sounds.

Noun	Verb	Way of representing the sound in writing or speech
car	rev	Vroom!
dog	bark	Woof!
nose	snore	ZZZZZZZZZZZZZ
fist/jaw	hit	Pow!
object/water	splash	Plop!
		Kerplop!
object flying quickly past		Swoosh!
someone	sail, zip	Whizz!

2.3

LEVEL
Any

TIME
Individual applications of this technique usually take only 10 seconds or so

MATERIALS
Optional: an audio or video recording

FOCUS
Intensive listening

WHAT WAS THAT?

Introducing the thread

1 Speak or play a cassette of a dialogue, or other text, for a short while.
2 Stop speaking or stop the recording and ask, 'What was that?' Students try to recall the word just said and repeat it to you. In a mixed-ability class, stop (at least some of the times) after a clearly stressed word. Ask less proficient students what the word was before asking more proficient students.

From lesson to lesson

→ Gradually begin to make a habit of asking students to repeat longer and longer chunks of language. In mixed-ability classes, encourage more proficient students to repeat more than just the single preceding word even when introducing this thread.

→ Ask more proficient students, 'How else could the speaker have said that?'

RATIONALE

- This technique is good, in short bursts, for waking your students up and getting them to pay attention.
- For you, it can be a useful check of listening comprehension.
- Those who haven't heard or understood something can learn from those who have.

THEY LISTEN FOR DIFFERENCES, THEN REMEMBER

They listen for differences, then remember is a sequence of tasks for use after students have already read or heard a text at least once and have understood its gist. All the elements of this activity have been floating around EFL for years. We find, though, that a surprising number of teachers either haven't met them or tend to forget that they have. Anyway, if you asked for an activity that never fails, this would be among the first that Seth would think of.

The basic idea is to use a written text, or the transcript of a listening text, in a way that has students reading and listening simultaneously. The text you use can be any kind of reading text between about 100 and 500 words long.

We find that this activity is particularly useful as a means of making up for what we think is an imbalance of emphasis in many recently published coursebooks. That is, while there may be lots of good texts both in the book and on the cassette, there are rarely enough *intensive* reading or listening tasks. As a result, teachers often seem to feel it necessary to keep telling their classes, 'It doesn't matter if you haven't understood everything.' Really? It doesn't matter to who? Gist reading and writing tasks are valuable. However, before students move on from a text to something new, they almost always want an opportunity to understand it in some detail. It's very likely to be quite demotivating to students in the long run if texts are too often exploited only at gist level. This activity is a good, quick way of satisfying students' natural desire to understand more of what they read and hear in class. After all, it's frustrating enough for learners not to understand much of what they hear on TV and radio, in films and so on. It seems perverse not to help them understand as much as possible of what's in their own coursebooks.

Preparation

1 The first couple of times you do this you might want to go through your chosen text the night before. Decide if it's liable to be challenging for your group or not. If the text is liable to be quite linguistically challenging and if it's longer than about 150 words, then choose a passage from the text of that length. If it's not very linguistically challenging for your class, you can cover as many as 300 words or so. (Advanced students can cope with up to 400, depending on the text and topic.)

2.4

LEVEL
Elementary – Advanced

TIME
5–20 minutes

MATERIALS
A short text

FOCUS
Intensive listening; correspondence between written and spoken language; paraphrasing

2 On your copy of the text (but not on theirs!) underline the words and short phrases you want to paraphrase. (See the examples below.) These can be of two kinds:

- ones your students already understand
- ones you think might be new to your students.

It's especially important that your paraphrases for both kinds of vocabulary are easy for your students to understand. The motto here is, 'Make the text clearer for them, not foggier.'

3 Mentally plan your paraphrases.

Introducing the thread

1 Tell the class that you're going to ask them how many two to four word phrases they can recall from the text (or, if it's a long text, from the first paragraph). Give them a half-minute or so to read the text. (Remember, you're using a text (e.g. in their casebook) that they've already worked with a bit.) Answer any questions about easy-to-explain vocabulary. If an explanation would take you more than a few seconds, say that you'll be explaining that point in a couple of minutes.

2 Tell students to turn over their sheets. Ask them to call out the phrases they remember. When they stop chiming in, ask them to look quickly at their texts and try to locate the various phrases that were mentioned.

3 Explain that you are going to read the text out loud but will sometimes use words that are different from the ones they see before them but which mean the same. When you do, they should underline that part of the text.

4 Do one sentence as a trial and check they all understand what to do. Then read through the text, paraphrasing as you go. Read at a speed that is somewhat challenging, but not impossibly fast. You must definitely not give them time to note down your paraphrases.

5 Form pairs and ask them to compare what they've underlined. Also (without having warned them about this beforehand) ask them to try to remember and then note down what you actually did say instead of what they've underlined. This will probably strike them as impossible, but in fact most students remember almost everything, provided you haven't used paraphrases that contain new language.

6 When most pairs have finished, ask if anyone wants to ask you what any of your paraphrases were. Write up a framework such as, 'In paragraph . . . line . . ., what did you say instead of . . .?'

From lesson to lesson

→ Use longer and longer texts.
→ Speak at an increasingly natural speed, use contractions where it would be natural to do so in speaking, etc.

→ Replace specific lexis (e.g. *mansion, stroll*) with general lexis (e.g. *house, walk*).

→ Replace general lexis (e.g. *hold*) with specific lexis (e.g. *grip*).

→ Move from paraphrasing single words to replacing longer and longer phrases.

→ Change passives to actives.

→ Change actives to passives.

→ Change reported speech to direct speech.

→ Change direct speech to reported speech.

→ Focus on changes of register. For example, consistently make changes that make a text more formal.

→ Insert words that aren't in the text at all. Students make slashes (i.e. '/') to mark the inserts.

→ Change word order. For example, instead of *Sometimes this happens* say *This happens sometimes*. Students draw arrows to show the shifts.

→ When teaching upper-level *one-to-one* students, ask them to be 'teacher'. As you report the changes you remember, give some feedback on their appropriateness.

Example text (intermediate) followed by example paraphrases

Police unlock riddle of missing boot boy By Paul Stokes

Frantic father Mr Owen Morse drove around streets near his home for 90 minutes looking for his five-year-old son Michael, *unaware* that he was locked in the car boot all the time.

As he searched *in vain*, Welsh police *mounted a hunt* with tracker dogs. Michael *attempted* to *raise the alarm* by *banging* his head and hands *inside* the boot and shouting during his *five-hour ordeal*.

But *his cries went unheeded* until PC Alwyn Trevor, one of the searching officers, suggested that Mr Morse check his car. When Morse, 32, *lifted the boot lid* of his blue Fiat Regatta, Michael's face *peered* up at him. As his mother, Mrs Megan Morse, 33, lifted him out in her arms, Michael told her, 'Dad drives at a hell of a speed.'

Michael said he had climbed into the boot to dry off after getting his green tracksuit trousers and red polo-neck *jumper* wet in the rain. But the lid *slammed shut* as he played at kicking it up and down.

Mr and Mrs Morse called in police after checking the places where Michael *normally* played and the homes of his friends.

Mr Morse, a builder, of Bro Teigi, Cardigan, Dyfed, said yesterday, 'I had no idea Michael was so *near*. I was *out of my mind with* worry. I drove everywhere I could think of to search for him, but *there was no sign*. The noise of the engine must have *drowned out* the noises he was making in the boot. I must have been back to the house five times. I had just *arrived* back at the house *yet again* when a police officer suggested I look in the boot. I thought there was no *point in* that. You can imagine my surprise when I saw Michael there. It was as if a *great* weight just *dropped* from my shoulders.'

The Daily Telegraph 5.10.93, p. 6.

unaware → He didn't know
in vain → without success
mounted a hunt → began to look
attempted → tried
raise the alarm → let people know he was in difficulty
banging . . . inside → hitting . . . against
five-hour ordeal → difficult five-hour experience
his cries went unheeded → nobody reacted to his cries
lifted the boot lid → opened the door of the boot
peered → looked
jumper → pullover/sweater
slammed shut → closed with a bang*
normally → usually
near → nearby
out of my mind with → frantic**
there was no sign → I couldn't see him
drowned out → hidden/covered over
arrived → got back
yet again → one more time
point in → reason for
great → heavy
dropped → fallen

*Since *banging* has been paraphrased above, it should be OK to use *bang* here; in fact it might be a bit of useful repetition.
**This glosses *frantic*, which occurs as the first word in the text but is difficult to accurately and simply paraphrase there.

COMMENT
This is about the right density of paraphrases. Incidentally, it's a good idea at some point to explain (1) that your paraphrases express the meaning of vocabulary as used *in this context* and (2) that in different contexts some of the vocabulary might be paraphrased differently.

2.5

WHAT'S COMING NEXT?

LEVEL
Any

Introducing the thread

TIME
Individual applications of this technique usually take only 10 seconds or so

1 Speak, or play a recording of a dialogue, or other kind of text, for a short while.
2 Stop speaking or stop the recording and ask, 'What word comes next?' It can be particularly useful to stop before the end of a collocation. Take, for example, the sentence 'So, the next night they all jumped in the car and went for a . . .' Stop here.
3 Students make suggestions. *Drive/joyride/drink/Chinese meal* are all completions of the form *go for a X*.

From lesson to lesson

→ Ask for two words, eventually three, and so on.
→ If you manage to elicit exactly what comes next, ask for alternative wordings.

RATIONALE

- This technique keeps students on their toes.
- It is good for consolidation and review of syntax, vocabulary and collocations.

MATERIALS
Optional: an audio or video recording

FOCUS
Intensive listening

WHICH WORDS DID YOU HEAR?

Introducing the thread

1 Speak or play a short sentence or bit of text. Beforehand, ask students to remember or note down the stressed words *only*. For example, (assuming neutral stressing):
   - beginner: *Where do you live?*→*Where, live*
   - lower intermediate: *So I went out and bought it for myself*→*went out* (or just *out*), *bought, myself* (or just *self*).
   - advanced: use recordings of, e.g. snippets of quick dialogue.
2 Ask students to make a sentence using the stressed words in the same order. If they remember your exact words, fine; if not, that's fine too. Don't expect lower-level students to be grammatically accurate.
3 Students write their sentences on the board and you write up the original utterance, on the board. Discuss any interesting differences between it and the students' sentences.

RATIONALE

- This is good for helping students to see that hearing the *stressed* words often amounts to getting much or all of the most important information.
- Also, practice not only improves performance at inferring the bits between the stressed 'landmarks', but also brings improvement in students' abilities actually to hear these unstressed bits.

ACKNOWLEDGEMENT
Tessa learnt this from Paul Vermes in the seventies.

2.6

LEVEL
Any

TIME
Individual applications of this technique usually take a minute or two

MATERIALS
Optional: an audio or video recording

FOCUS
Listening for stressed words

2.7

LEVEL
Elementary –
Upper
intermediate

TIME
5–10 minutes

MATERIAL
A challenging
listening text, rich
in different
categories of
information

FOCUS
Listening for
important details
of subject matter

WHO, WHAT, WHERE, WHEN?

Introducing the thread

1 Read out or play a recording of a story, or tune in to a news bulletin with students. Ask students to make headings in their notebooks like this:

People   Times   Places   Numbers   Happenings

2 On the first listening, deal with the *first* column *only*. Before students hear the text for the first time, ask them to listen for all the words having to do with people, for example, *she, the group, the president, the miners*. After the first listening, elicit what everyone has heard and write this on the board under the appropriate heading.

3 Before reading out or playing the text a second time, ask the less proficient students to listen for the items they missed the first time (i.e. people). Suggest they listen out for the items listed on the board. Ask the more proficient to listen out only for times, for example, *yesterday, at five o'clock, later today, next, before*. After the second listening, list what they've heard in the 'Times' column on the board.

4 During the third hearing, the less proficient listen for the items listed in the 'Times' column on the board. The more proficient go on to listen only for places. Ask those who need a special challenge to listen out for whole prepositional phrases, for example, *at the airport, in Zagreb, in their front room*.

5 Continue working in this way so that the lower proficiency students are always trying to recognise things already listed.

6 Ask people to try to construct the story from all the information they have noted in the different columns. If your students want, finish by reading or playing the text one last time.

From lesson to lesson

Once the first four columns have been filled in, ask them to fill in the 'Happenings' column too before they listen again.

RATIONALE

This technique allows you to use quite different listening texts (particularly authentic ones) with groups of students, some or all of whom are not proficient enough to cope without plenty of help. Success in comprehending a difficult piece of listening material, such as news broadcasts, can be a great confidence builder, especially in the case of lower-level learners.

CATCHING ENGLISH OUT OF THE AIR

2.8

LEVEL
Elementary –
Advanced

TIME
From 1 to 20
minutes,
depending on
level and
concentration
ability of your
students

MATERIALS
Stretches of
authentic speech,
either recorded or
live

FOCUS
Helping students
to learn new ways
of saying things in
the target
language

Use any of the previous threads 2.2–2.7, separately or in combination, to give students practice in concentrating intently while listening. Now, the time has come to switch the focus from listening to what *you* wish students to listen for, to encouraging them to listen to what *they* are interested in.

Preparation

Invite in a visitor who is a native-speaker; or think of a topic you can talk to your students about with enthusiasm; or set up a tape of authentic speech. Plan how you will allow students to hear the text in segments of a minute or two in length. For example, if you're going to invite a speaker, how will you get them to break up their talk?

Introducing the thread

1 Tell students they are going to hear some authentic speech divided up into segments. Tell them about how long each segment will be. Ask them to listen out for any phrase or pattern that (a) interests them, (b) they don't understand but would like to, (c) (for low level learners) is exactly what they would say, (d) is slightly different from what they would say. Tell them that once they have 'caught' a phrase, they need to note it down so they don't forget it. If the phrase is new to them, it's quite possible they'll note it down incorrectly. This doesn't matter for the time being. Ask them to note down one thing from each of the segments they hear.

2 Students listen to the first segment.

3 Afterwards, allow students time to think and make notes. If necessary, allow them a second listening. Check whether everyone has written something down. If anyone hasn't, gently make sure that it's because nothing they heard was new or interesting to them.

4 Students listen to the next segment. Again, allow some time afterwards for note-taking.

5 Repeat this procedure until you come to the end of the planned listening.

6 Ask students what they have noted down. Write these phrases on the board in the order in which they occurred in the discourse. Answer any questions students ask. You may have to write up useful questions, e.g. *Is that correct/natural?*, *Do you often hear people say this?*, *Does it mean . . . ?*, *What does it mean?*, *When do you say it?*.

7 Ask students why they picked their phrases out of all the language they heard. Accept any reason, e.g. 'It sounds funny' or 'I just like it'.

From lesson to lesson

Over a series of lessons, encourage students to:
→ listen to longer and longer stretches of authentic speech
→ catch more phrases each time
→ ask more questions about usage (register, tone, etc.) and to make notes on what they learn about the usage of their phrases
→ use the phrases/patterns that interest them.

RATIONALE

- When students start thinking in this way (and they do), they become more and more able to scan authentic speech for vocabulary and patterns that interest them. They become able to gain input from any authentic source. Thus, any chat with a native speaker, any visit to the cinema or evening spent with a radio can become valuable for new language acquisition as well as for communication, for content learning or for vague 'listening practice'.
- Exposure to comprehensible input is thought to be of basic importance in second language acquisition. This activity adds a conscious, attentive, effortful element to such exposure.

ACKNOWLEDGEMENT
Thanks to Mario Rinvolucri for pioneering this way of listening on an advanced course for non-native-speaker teachers in Canterbury in the mid-1980s.

CHAPTER 3

Knowledge

This chapter contains threads designed to help students build and share their knowledge of all kinds of things: – the natural world (3.3 and 3.4), history, sports, cars and more. These threads allow simple and natural development of content teaching. This means that you regularly take time with your class to explore something of interest to them while *using* English rather than concentrating on it as a subject. Content teaching need not necessarily mean dealing with familiar school subjects like History and Geography. It can also mean:

- discussing good news items from the back pages of newspapers (e.g. 'New operations enabling deaf people to hear again', 'The resettlement of bears in their natural habitat')
- learning the names of the planets
- taking an old-fashioned clock to pieces, discussing the functions of different parts and then putting them back together again
- growing a bean plant in the classroom and weaving talk about its progress into the early minutes of occasional lessons.

ABBREVIATIONS AND SYMBOLS

Preparation

Choose a small number of abbreviations, symbols or acronyms that occur frequently in the target culture (say three to five items). Try to choose ones your students particularly need to know or ones which are in an area of interest to (some of) them.

Introducing the thread

1 Write the chosen items on the board. See if anyone knows them. If not, tell people what they mean, how to say them, what they stand for, when they are used, etc.
2 Give students practice in reading them out loud (e.g. in saying 'bee bee see' for *BBC*, not, e.g. 'double bee see', or 'three inches', not just 'three in' for *3 in*).

3.1

LEVEL
Elementary+

TIME
5 minutes+

MATERIALS
None

FOCUS
Recognising abbreviations, acronyms and symbols; reading them out loud; knowing what they stand for and when to use them

From lesson to lesson

→ Review items done previously and teach more items in the same area(s) (e.g. money, time) or move on to another area (e.g. dimension). Here are some target items divided up by topic:

Money
p	£	£8–£10
$	c	

Length
in/ins	ft	2'2"	10' x 6'	yd	m (=mile)
mm	cm	m	km		

Area
sq in	sq ft		
cm^2	m^2	h	km^2

Liquid content/capacity
fl oz	pt	qt	gal
ml cl	cc	dcl	l

Weight
oz	lb	16 st
gm	kg	

Temperature
75°F   −5°C

Maths
$+$ $-$ $\div$ $\times$ $=$ $\%$ 3^2 ¾   1½   2.2

Dates and time
Jan, Feb, etc.
M, T, W, Mon, Tues, etc.
Jan. 1st 1998, 1st Jan. 1998, 1 Jan. 1998, 1/1/98
8 a.m. 6 p.m. 6.30 18.30

Addresses and phone numbers
St	Rd	Ave	Sq	Cl	Cres	Dr	Blvd	Gdns	Pk
UK	GB	USA	CAN	AUS	NZ				

081–634–9024

Miscellaneous
mpg	mph	OK	approx	VIP	WC	PTO	ASAP
PO	RSVP	IOU	VAT				

Latinisms
e.g.	i.e.	etc.	PS	PPS	*c.*	NB	p.a.	ER	pp

Companies/Organisations
BR	BBC	ITV	C4	GPO	RAF	TUC	NUS	EC	UN	NATO

Other topics

- Abbreviations in advertisements for jobs, flats and houses, items for sale, lonely hearts columns, etc.
- Abbreviations in particular sciences, technologies, trades, sports (e.g. horseriding: TBX, 15.3hh, BHS, XC).

TEACHING DEFINITION SKILLS

3.2

LEVEL
Elementary+

TIME
15–25 minutes to introduce the thread at elementary level (less at higher levels)

MATERIALS
(Optional): For introducing the thread, a dozen or so photos; Blu-tack

FOCUS
Noticing and remembering basic definition strategies; learning and using the grammatical patterns involved; becoming aware of basic standards of informativeness; becoming useful in helping other students with vocabulary; increasing the use of English in the classroom for real communication

Elementary students, not surprisingly, are seldom able to produce a definition of any kind that is fully grammatical. Even advanced students are typically weak at defining words. They may, for example, appear not to have the slightest idea how to begin, just like some people can't give directions. At all levels students' definitions often seem unintelligible to their classmates.

Although this thread is particularly useful in preparing students for academic discourse, its main purpose is to make students of any or no specialisation better able to offer fellow-students *definitions that work against the background of what is going on in a particular time and place*. Not perfect, dictionary-like definitions, but effective ones that can be uttered fairly *ad lib*.

In the real world, effective definitions can be incomplete, unlike those in a dictionary which must be complete enough to help people who are looking up a word for which they have (or remember) little or no context. As it happens, giving a comprehensive, well-rounded definition of a word is often not so easy even for a native speaker. Could you quickly provide an all-around definition of *to show* for example? Luckily though, an incomplete definition, if it is linked to the context in which the word has come up, may work very well, particularly for someone who had learned the target item once before but has just had a lapse of memory. Here are some examples of potentially effective partial definitions of *to show*: 'Maite showed us some photographs'. 'The opposite of *hide*' or 'I want you to see this so I show it to you' (with gesture). We have seen all of these work in different classrooms. (Note that we use the word *definition* in its broadest sense to include anything someone says or does in order to clarify the meaning of vocabulary.)

Introducing the thread (at elementary level)

Make a list of the defining strategies you want your class to be able to use by the end of your course. The list below is a fairly extensive one. Instead of drawing ideas from our list, however, you can ask native speakers to define words of different kinds and record how they go about it. Do you notice recurring patterns?

Plan to introduce the patterns, or defining strategies, in your normal way.

Defining strategies
a For a thing, show or point to it: (*forehead*) 'This is my forehead.'
b Draw it. Thus, for *roof*, sketch a house and say, 'This is the roof.'
c Use gesture. Thus, for *roof*, show the shape of a typical North European roof with your hands and say, 'Roof'.
d Demonstrate. So, for *hop*, hop and say, 'This is hopping.'
e Make a representative noise. Thus, for *explode*, shout, 'BOOM! . . . . Explode'.

If your students have learned a couple of hundred 'basic kind' nouns and a corresponding number of adjectives, begin introducing strategies (f)–(q). (Basic kind nouns are ones like *snake, cat, car, milk, house* which native-speaking children tend to learn before corresponding 'specific-level nouns' such as *cobra, Burmese, coupé, skimmed milk, shack* and 'general-level nouns' like *reptile, mammal, vehicle, liquid, dwelling*.)

f For a kind, say what the next highest class is:
(*wolf*) 'A wolf is a kind of wild dog.'
g For a class, give examples of things it includes:
(*mammal*) 'Dogs are mammals; cats and cows and elephants are too.'
h For parts, name the whole:
(*roof*) 'A roof is a part of a house.'

The reverse of this, defining the term for a whole by listing parts seems not to be used very often in classroom talk since if we know the names of the parts we probably know the word for the whole. (e.g. *house*: 'A house has a roof and doors.') On the other hand, this strategy is typical of academic writing when terms are being defined.

i For an ingredient, say what you can make with it:
(*flour*) 'You make bread with flour. Bread is almost all flour.'
j For products, name an ingredient or two:
(*cider*) 'You make cider from apples.'
k For job and place nouns, name some typical actions or activities:
(*designer*) 'A designer is a person who makes a picture of a machine before the machine is made.'
(*brewery*) 'A brewery is a place where people make beer.'
l If a thing has a function, say what it is:
(*roof*) 'A roof is for keeping wind and rain out of a house and for keeping warm air in.'
m If a thing is not difficult to describe, describe it:
(*tiger*) 'Tigers are orangish cats and they have black stripes. Some are more than three metres long.'
n Say where it can be found:
(*pastry*) 'You can find pastry in a bakery.'
o For a place, say what you can find there:
(*orchard*) 'An orchard is where you find fruit trees.'

p Give a synonym, paraphrase or antonym:
- '*Reply* means "answer".'
- '*Huge* means "very big".'
- 'The opposite of *huge* is *tiny*.'

Move on to the following strategies:

q For a process, describe its input and output:
(*fermentation*) 'Fermentation is a process whereby sugar is turned into alcohol.'

r Give a cause:
(*wet*) 'If you fall into water, you get wet.'

s Give a result:
(*puncture*) 'If you puncture a tyre, the air comes out.'

t Describe an instance (especially for verbs and verbal nouns):
(*vault*) 'Vaulting is when you jump over something and use a pole or one of your hands to help yourself get over.'

u Give connotations:
(*shifty*) 'If you call someone shifty, you really don't like them.'

v Comment on other limitations on use:
'That's American English/old-fashioned/slang/very technical . . .'

From lesson to lesson

→ Get students to use the strategies they've been exposed to by encouraging them to define words for each other.

→ Keep on display a poster bearing a record of the strategies already taught. If a student appears not to remember which strategy they can use, point to the poster.

→ Guessing games can provide review of strategies and component grammatical patterns, e.g.

Student: It's a person who works long hours.
Class: A taxi driver
Student: Good guess, but wrong. It's a person who usually doesn't earn much money.

(Rules: Each guess must be commented on and a new clue must be given after each wrong guess.)

→ Ask students to make crossword puzzles with clues in the form of partial definitions, for example: 'For sitting on'.

→ Present and practise ways of combining strategies, especially in writing. For example: 'A tiger is a kind of wild cat. Tigers live in Asia, mostly in India. They are orangish and have black stripes.' This is especially important for students with academic aspirations.

Advanced level:

→ Variations on the defining game 'Call My Bluff' can be fun and useful provided that your students have had sufficient practice beforehand in forming definitions. The basic idea is as follows.

1 Members of one team tell members of another team a few new words and a definition for each. At least one of the words has a definition taken from a dictionary and at least one has a made-up definition.

2 The opposing teams try to guess which definitions are false. The winning team is the one that has fooled the opposition most often.

3.3

LEVEL
Beginner – Upper intermediate

TIME
1–5 minutes

MATERIALS
Optional: pictures of animals

FOCUS
Building vocabulary

WHAT'VE WE GOT? WHAT'VE THEY GOT?

Preparation

Ask students to set aside a dozen or so pages in their notebooks for notes on 'body parts' and 'animals'.

Introducing the thread (at beginner level)

1 Every lesson or so, teach one or two new words for basic parts of the human body: *head, arm, leg, eye, nose, hair,* etc.

2 When students have learned a dozen or so key words, make the change to animals. Begin by drawing on the board a sketch of an animal that shows some of the body parts already taught. (Or show a picture and then stick it onto the board.) Elicit words for some of the body parts of the animal and ask students to come to the board and draw arrows and labels (see Fig. 12).

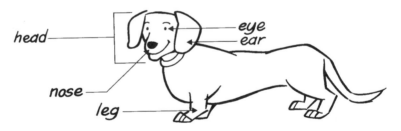

Figure 12 A partly labelled dog

3 Elicit or teach one to three new words, ones for body parts the animal has but we don't. For a dog, that might be *tail* and *fur*.

From lesson to lesson

→ Introduce new animals, e.g. a typical fish (*fins* and *scales*), a typical bird (*wings, feathers* and *beak*), a duck (*webbed feet* and *bill*), a cat (*claws* and *whiskers*), a turtle (*shell*). Encourage students to enter new vocabulary into the section of their notebooks mentioned in 'Preparation' above.

→ Keep reviewing previous learning. For example, if you've done six animals already, review three one day, and review a different three the next.

→ Add in other parts of speech, e.g. link *to claw* to *a claw*.

→ With higher-level students, teach or elicit more complex terms. Thus, for a cat, you might aim for *feet, stripes, green eyes* or *claws* with low-proficiency students and *paws, tabby markings, eyes that see in the dark* or *retractable claws* with higher-proficiency students.

→ Introduce students to wider applications of 'body part' and 'animal' words. What else can have a head? (A company, a bed . . .) A foot? (A mountain, a bed . . .) Legs? (Tables, chairs . . .) Wings? (Planes, large buildings . . .) A tongue? (A shoe . . .) Eyes? (Hurricanes, needles . . .) Claws? (Hammers, crabs . . .) Fins? (Fifties American cars . . .) Scales? (Human skin can be scaly; taps and kettles can be scaled up.) People can *waddle* or *croak*. And so on.

→ Emphasize the versatility of animal words by presenting/eliciting examples of metaphorical use, e.g. 'Creditors try to claw back their loans'.

→ Add new 'questions'. Again, work with vocabulary appropriate to the different levels of student in your class. Ask, e.g.:

- What are they like? (*cold, wet, furry, wild, tame, slimy*)
- Where do they live? (*in the water, in trees, on river banks, on and near water*)
- What do they do? (*swim, build nests, fly, catch mice*)
- How do they move? (*fly, swim, paddle and waddle*)
- What noise to they make? (*miaow, purr, howl*)
- What do they live on? (*dogfood, insects, worms*)
- Where do they sleep? (*on sofas, in nests*)

→ Go with your students' interests. If you think they're not interested in animal words, do everyday things (e.g. shoes, clocks), modes of transport (plane, coach, bicycle, ferry), appliances . . . whatever.

→ Be prepared to adapt to individual interests. Thus, if a student is a shoe manufacturer, do shoes (*toe, heel, tongue, eyelet, sole, last, seam*).

3.4

LEVEL
Lower
intermediate+

TIME
1–10 minutes

MATERIALS
A picture or
example of the
thing to be
focused on

FOCUS
Building
vocabulary;
exemplifying the
meaning and use
of *do for* and *do
to*.

WHAT CAN WE DO FOR EACH OTHER?

Introducing the thread (at intermediate level)

Bring in a living thing, a plant perhaps. Ask, 'What can we do for it?'
Elicit responses. From less proficient students accept brief suggestions (e.g. 'Give it water'). Encourage more proficient students to give
more detail (e.g. 'Give it water, but not too much', 'Put it in the sunlight, but not for too long', 'Put it in a bigger pot'). Help students with
pronunciation. Perhaps write their ideas on the board. If you elicit
more than three suggestions or so, don't suggest any yourself. Give
one or two ideas yourself if students are not so forthcoming.

From lesson to lesson

→ Introduce new examples in the same category (e.g. for living
things: a goldfish, wild bird, a parrot, a tree, an earthworm, a
penguin, a mosquito, a friend who's hungry.)

→ Review previous learning. Perhaps ask if anyone has had, in the
meantime, any new ideas about what we could do for a plant, say.
Or ask people to mime helpful actions that have come up before
and see if others can guess them.

→ Introduce new questions, for example: 'What do . . . do for us?'
(e.g. cows: give us milk; elephants: carry us; birds: cheer us up
with their songs.)

Intermediate level:

→ In mature groups, you can make a change to thinking about inan-
imate objects (e.g. bottles, paper clips, bits of wood, pieces of fur-
niture) and materials (e.g. paper, cloth, leather, plastic).

1 Explain the difference between do to and do with. That is, doing
something to something often involves a change in the thing
(perhaps damage). Doing something with something means that
you use it as a tool or device in order to accomplish something else.

2 Hand out sheets of scrap paper. Ask, 'What can we do to paper?'
Ask someone to show you one action. If no one does, demonstrate
by, for example, making a little tear. Elicit or teach the word.

3 Ask students to do things to the paper. Set a time limit of fifteen
seconds or so. Teach or elicit the English words.

4 Correct errors and deal with pronunciation. If students know quite
a few words, don't teach any new ones yourself.

5 Next time, review 'old' words and add one or two new ones. Among
the words you can choose from in regard to paper, depending on
the level, are *tear off a corner, fold, crease, dog-ear, tear, rip, crumple,
twist, dent, puncture* . . .

KNOW-HOW

Introducing the thread

LEVEL
Upper
elementary+

TIME
A few minutes+

MATERIALS
None

FOCUS
Sharing know-how
with other
students; talking
about topics they
know something
about

1 Ask a question to which you know the answer because you have gained expertise through experience with the matter. Example questions are:

- How can you stop a baby from crying?
- How can you keep a company from losing money?
- How can you get an unwilling horse into a horse box (i.e. horse van)?
- How can you get an unwilling horse to cross a bridge?
- How can you train a dog to follow you at your heels?
- How can you train a dog to stop chasing sheep?
- How can you get stains out of clothing?
  Choose one question.
2 Students brainstorm ideas to solve this 'riddle'.
3 As students come up with ideas, polish the wording if need be and then get them to repeat their ideas in a reasonably natural form and fashion. Write the ideas up on the board as you go along (perhaps in a scatter pattern here and there rather than in neatly stacked lines).

From lesson to lesson

→ Invite a student to ask the rest of the class their own 'How can you . . .?' question based on expertise that they personally possess.

If you have a group of people who like brainteasers, try questions which are a bit more like riddles. Ask one per lesson, e.g.

- When snow melts, where does the white go? (Answer: Into the air. That is, the whiteness of snow is trapped air; the air escapes when the snow turns to water.)
- Why are fleas thin? (So they can move about easily between hairs.)
- Why doesn't the weather turn warmer when the days start getting longer? (Because the days are still so much shorter than the nights that the hemisphere in question continues to lose heat into space. This goes on more or less until the days become longer than the nights.)
- How can a tree be a climate control device for a house? (If it's deciduous, it can shade the house in summer and let through the sun in winter.)
- Why are fish almost always dark on top and white on the bottom? (So that, when seen from above they can be camouflaged against the darkness of the bottom and when seen from below they won't stand out so much against the brightness of the sky.)
- Why is it more hygienic to let dishes drain than to dry them with a cloth? (Using a cloth spreads bacteria from one plate to another.)

Don't ask for answers on the spot. Instead, say that you will ask for (oral) answers in the next lesson. In the following lesson, invite people to answer. Be careful about rejecting answers even if they're clearly wrong. If someone suggests the answer you had in mind, say something like, 'Well, that seemed like the answer to me too.' Don't say, 'That's right' or 'Good!' If no one comes up with a plausible answer, ask them if they want another day or few days to think or if they want to hear what you think the answer is. Pose a new question for the following lesson.

→   From time to time ask, 'Who can remember how to . . .?' or 'Why was it that . . .?'

→   Pose questions that require longer, more detailed answers. Note that 'scientific' questions (e.g. 'How are rainbows formed?') often take too long to explain even if people do happen to know the answer and their English is good enough. Such questions may be suitable for some ESP (English for Special Purposes) groups, though.

→   Students write two- or three-line problems, exchange them, write replies and return them. Stress that these can be less puzzling than the examples given above. Something like, 'Why do ducks have webbed feet?' is fine.

CHAPTER 4

Seeing clearly

The lesson band 'seeing clearly' consists of a suite of threads working on the visual sense. Students' (and your) observation of detail is improved and the everyday visual material available in all classrooms is used as a springboard to vocabulary building and fluency practice.

WHAT'S THE WEATHER LIKE TODAY?

This idea only works if you're teaching in a country with varied weather: an island country like Britain, perhaps, or a place near mountains!

Introducing the thread

You begin by asking, 'What's the weather like today?' Aim to build up students' repertoires of vocabulary and structures over a few lessons under headings such as these:

a *It's*+adjective (e.g. *sunny, cloudy, windy, wet, dry, dull, awful out, cold, crisp, bleak, gloomy, depressing*)

b *It's*+verb+-*ing* (e.g. *raining, drizzling*)

c *It's*+comparative (e.g. *better than/the same as yesterday*)

d *It's*+adverb+adjective e.g. *quite, a bit, rather, very, absolutely*

e *There's a/some/a lot of . . .* (e.g. *fog, cloud, east wind/wind coming from the east*)

f *You can see . . .* (e.g. *the trees moving, as far as X, huge clouds*)

g Clichés (e.g. *lovely weather for ducks, this is probably our summer today, you know what they say about our weather – if you don't like it just wait a few minutes, summer around here is one month of bad sledging*)

h *The main colours (of the sky, foliage, clouds,* etc.*) are . . .*

i *This sort of weather/day reminds me of . . .*

j *I wouldn't want to . . . in this weather*

k The vocabulary of keen weather watchers (e.g. *a mackerel sky, cumulo-nimbus, cirrus, isobars, Force 8 gale*)

In mixed-ability classes, encourage less proficient students to come up with ideas in the (a) and (b) groups and stretch more proficient students by helping them to move on to descriptions in the (f)–(k) groups.

4.1

LEVEL
Any

TIME
A couple of minutes+

MATERIALS
None

FOCUS
Building vocabulary; enabling students to converse about a common everyday topic

From lesson to lesson

→ At each use of the thread, add a few new ones and keep going until students are able to spontaneously give full, accurate and varied descriptions.

→ Watch or listen to TV or radio weather forecasts. Play recordings of ordinary people discussing the weather.

→ Students describe the weather through the eyes of different people, for example: a farmer, a windsurfer, a house painter, an airline pilot, a sea captain, a lorry driver, a skier, a nudist, a poet.

→ If your classes are taking place in a country where there are lots of native speakers of English, ask students to survey one or two native speakers each by asking, 'How would you describe the weather today if you were a farmer? A windsurfer?', etc. In a later class, students report (1) the commonest responses and (2) the most interesting responses.

4.2

LEVEL
Any

TIME
5–10 minutes

MATERIALS
None

FOCUS
Building vocabulary; developing a sense of adjective order; developing a sense of when to use the Present Simple and the Present Continuous tenses; practising various other structures (see below)

WHAT ARE WE ALL WEARING?

Introducing the thread

Build up vocabulary under headings such as:
- names of garments and accessories (e.g. *a T-shirt*)
- colours (e.g. *a red T-shirt*)
- materials (e.g. *a red cotton T-shirt*)
- simple patterns (e.g. *a plain/striped red cotton T-shirt*)
- *with* phrases (e.g. *a cotton T-shirt with red and white stripes and a pocket*)
- other modifiers (e.g. *long, loose, baggy, straightleg, sheer, tight*)
- relative clauses (e.g. *the red cotton T-shirt (that) she often wears*)
- *it goes with/matches/suits . . . It would go with . . .* etc.
- Present Simple (*you usually wear a watch*) v Present Continuous (*you're wearing your hair differently today*).

In mixed-ability classes, lower-level students will be struggling with nouns, colours and word order, whilst higher-level students can be challenged to use more modifiers, relative clauses, etc.

From lesson to lesson

Some of this language can be practised through activities such as the following:

→ Say what a partner is wearing.

→ Say what a friend (not a classmate) usually wears.

→ 'Kim's Game With Clothes':

1 Students stand face to face in pairs, stare at each other's clothes for a minute, then turn around so they can't see each other.

2 From memory they say things like 'You're wearing . . .' 'You always/often wear a wedding ring/glasses/a gold chain.'

3 When Student A can't think of any other things Student B is wearing, Student B adds anything that was left out or corrects anything that was factually wrong.

→ 'You've Taken Off Your . . .!':

1 Same as Step 1 above.

2 Everyone makes two to four changes in their attire. For example, someone might turn up their collar, tuck a trouser leg into a sock, put their shoes on the wrong feet.

3 Students turn around, face each other and make statements like, 'You've pulled out your shirt-tail.'

→ 'That Would Go With My . . .':

1 Students mingle and stare at each other's attire.

2 Everyone sits down and calls out sentences like, 'X's pencil case would go with my T-shirt.'

→ As a continuation, or to start with, if your students wear uniforms, draw on other ways in which students express their personality such as different pencil cases, or the ways they make their book bags different from each other.

HOW MANY FRAMES?

Most people readily see why tigers and leopards, say, are deemed to belong to the class of *cat*. There are other less common terms (besides *cat, dog, fish, furniture,* etc.) which students may require some guidance with in order to understand – the class term *frame*, for example. However, once students do fully understand words like this, they find themselves in possession of powerful tools for naming and describing not only objects and structures, but ideas as well. This thread can help students see new structure and consistency in the world at large.

Introducing the thread

1 Ask if someone can point out a frame somewhere in the room. If no one can, point out one yourself, for example, a window frame. Get the students to repeat *window frame* with natural rhythm and intonation.

2 Say that there are several other kinds of frame in the room. Ask students to point them out and to try to guess their names. Most classrooms have at least one of the following: door frame, picture frame, board frame, glasses/spectacles frame.

4.3

LEVEL
Upper-elementary+

TIME
3–15 minutes

MATERIALS
None

FOCUS
Building vocabulary; developing awareness of the functions of a wide variety of objects and physical constructions

3 If students don't know the word *dimension*, teach it. If no one has yet pointed out any three-dimensional frames, tell them that some frames have three dimensions – glasses frames, for example. Someone may now point out that chairs can have frames. This might be a good time to pause and teach or elicit a preliminary definition of a *frame*, e.g. 'Something that goes around something else and holds it together, keeps it from falling down, over, out; or holds it up.' If you have handy a chair with a visible frame, ask someone to point to those parts of the chair that are not part of the frame (e.g. the cushions). Distinguish between frames on the one hand and stands (as for a lamp or a television) and legs on the other. Some tables, for example, have legs but no frames.

4 Ask if frames can ever be just for decoration. Do they see any like this in the room? Have they ever seen any like this? Where? Differentiate between frames and margins, borders and frills. (Frames always at least *look* like they have some structural function.)

5 Add that some frames hold things up from the inside, rather than from the outside. Ask if people have frames like this. What are they made of? (Bone.) What do we generally call them? (Skeletons.)

6 Ask what else – outside the room – has frames. (Cars; and some buildings have frames of timbers or steel beams.)

From lesson to lesson

→ Review previous learning.

→ Refer increasingly to objects outside the room.

→ Introduce other parts of speech (e.g. *frame a picture*).

→ Introduce metaphorical extensions. For example, ask students to guess what a 'time frame' is. Then a 'mental frame'. Ask what you do if you 'frame a problem'. Explain the idiom *frame someone* (regarding a crime) ask students to say why *frame* might have been chosen for use in this idiom. And/or ask them to work in pairs to draw pictures of the idiom. (Some people are reluctant to draw but are good at suggesting what to draw.)

→ Repeat the idea with other functional objects or structures, e.g.:
  - *panel:* stiff, solid, flattish material, often inside a frame. Doors may have panels, a window pane is a kind of panel (note: *pane/panel*), your board is a kind of panel, stiff briefcases have side panels.
  - *handle:* there should be many of these about, for example: on the cassette player, on the television perhaps, on bags. Mention that we find handles on things we can pick up. Handles on things we don't pick up may have other names. Elicit some of these (e.g. *knob, railing, grip*). Ask the class to decide if handles tend to have a similar shape and size as opposed, for example, to knobs. Ask what things that are outside the classroom have handles.

- *cover/covering:* a covering is thinner than a cover, may have a broad expanse and may well adhere to the surface.
- *hook:* e.g. coat hooks, picture hooks.
- *hinge:* e.g. on a door, in a pair of glasses, the spine of a book, an elbow joint.

→ Many general terms are different from *frame* in that they are not usually used to refer to specific objects. *Container* is an example. Thus, while we say *window frame*, we usually say *milk bottle* not *milk container* (when we are speaking of a glass container with a narrow neck).

Class terms like *container* provide a good means of structuring the teaching of numerous high frequency nouns, e.g.:

- *container* (e.g. *palm of hand, pocket, pencil case, biro cartridge, flower pot, suitcase, petrol tank*).

→ One by one, tackle *join/connection, decoration, device, boundary.*

1 Elicit or teach a few specific terms first. For the class term *boundary*, for example, that could be *kerb, fence, hedge, seashore.* Elicit like this, for example:

Teacher: What do you find at the side of a street?
Student: Pavement.
Teacher: Yes. What about between the street and the pavement?

2 When you have elicited or taught a few examples of your class term (e.g. *boundary*), ask, 'Do you know a word for all of these things?' Or, 'All of these things are examples of what?' If no one knows the word (e.g. *boundary*) then teach it.

DRAWING AND LABELLING

This thread is popular with students of all levels but is especially useful to advanced learners.

Introducing the thread

1 On the board begin a drawing of your own face. Keep your drawing crude in order (1) to show poor drawers in the class that poor drawings will be good enough and (2) to shift attention from skill at drawing to the business of labelling. Pause after you've drawn in each new feature such as face or hair and elicit a label for it. Push students to come up with more than just a basic noun. So, if you've drawn an oval face, see if higher-level students can come up with *oval face*, ditto if you've drawn hair (*medium-length brown . . .*), etc. Or can they say *fringe* as well as just *hair*? The idea is that they should push themselves and move from what they know to what they don't know.

Even with a simple, rough sketch you should be able to elicit

4.4

LEVEL
Any

TIME
Variable

MATERIALS
(Optional): Large sheets of paper, coloured pens and pencils

FOCUS
Developing habits of keen observation; encouraging students to stretch themselves in vocabulary learning

plenty of labels from all but absolute beginners. Elementary learners will come out with nouns like *mouth, eyes, ears, nose, hair, face, glasses* . . . in addition to adjectives like *big, small, round* . . ., all of which you can build on.

2 Students form pairs and sit opposite each other. Tell them that now they are going to draw each other and label their sketches. Explain that there are three rules:

   a Every separate thing they draw – every part, every feature – must have a label. So, almost every time they add a new line, they will need to add a new label.

   b After labelling what they know, they must push themselves to add something they don't know, either a new noun (e.g. *earrings*) or a new modifier (e.g. *gold* . . ., or . . . *for pierced ears*).

   c You are the 'word waitress/waiter'. Students call you over for help anytime they like. You are unlikely to be rushed in this role as students will generally need your services at different times. For example, some will complete their drawing before beginning to label while others will label as they go along. Also, of course, they will be getting some help with vocabulary from each other.

3 Hand out coloured pens/pencils and sheets of paper and ask students to begin.

4 Students swap pictures, look and laugh. Since what they see is all about themselves, any new vocabulary is more likely to interest them and be remembered.

From lesson to lesson

In class:

→ Students draw and label various objects, even the most mundane. Demonstrate by looking together at something commonplace like the board (you'll see, e.g. chalk dust, a scratch, an aluminium ledge . . .) or the classroom door (with, e.g. metal hinges, cracked gloss paint, panels, an old-fashioned lock, a see-through keyhole . . .)

→ Students bring in more interesting objects for drawing and labelling.

As homework . . .

→ Ask students to draw and label something they all have at home (e.g. front door, sink, TV . . .) (the same thing for everyone). Set aside time in class the following lesson for students to show their drawings and ask about and add vocabulary they didn't know.

→ As they get more proficient at labelling, ask them to draw and label: favourite things (e.g., a bike, a pet . . .), something small and ordinary, something electrical, and so on.

COMMENT

- Of course students can make lists of the parts or features of things without drawing them, but the drawing powerfully stimulates concentration and attention to detail. The addition of colour makes a big difference too, which is why we suggest that for classroom drawing you bring in as many coloured pens and pencils as you can. Having large sheets of paper (e.g. A3) also helps. (Many of our students seem to favour pocket-sized notebooks which are not suitable for sketching in.)

- Students generally sit next to someone they feel more or less comfortable with. This diminishes any risk during student-student drawing of faces that student A might deliberately draw an unflattering picture of student B. A more effective control, though, is the fact that A knows that B is making a drawing too.

RATIONALE

The ultimate aim of this thread is for students to form the habit (any time they're bored) of drawing or visualising some object and seeing if they can label its parts and features in the target language. Thus, in the next stage of this thread, students come to a class with questions like 'What do you call this part of a . . .?' Ultimately, some of your students will carry on with this inquisitive, self-starting approach to vocabulary learning when they've finished with language courses and they're on their own.

CHAPTER 5

Reviewing

Here is one of our colleagues speaking about reviews:

'However great your teaching techniques are, they're absolutely wasted unless you have good review techniques as well. You can learn a language inside a classroom or outside on the street. In many ways, learning outside is superior but the two things that a classroom can offer are: (1) absolute clarity in presentation of form, meaning and use, and (2) consistent, systematic revision. I heard somewhere that you need to meet something seven times for it to move from short-term to long-term memory. I've also read that review is more efficient if it happens at certain times – for example, a swift recap at the end of a lesson, just after a lesson and then at longer and longer intervals. Part of that is up to the students, but what can the teacher do to help?

'Just after every lesson, I write down on a sheet of paper all the vocabulary, phrases, structures and areas of work that have come up in the lesson. That's what takes the time – that writing down. Then, at the start of the next lesson, for about six minutes, I play quiet, pleasant music and we do the review.

'I'll spot-check vocabulary by holding up pictures or reminding people of the themes of lessons. I use a lot of visuals: cue cards, pictures, charts, notes and prompts. Once a week we have a "mega-review". All the students have a copy of the review sheet. Then, in pairs, they make up questions for each other. It'll take about fifteen to twenty minutes. Let's say that there are ten new items per lesson. Then, after a while, you'd be up to about seventy items for review. But you don't check them all. Some will have sunk in fast and be known anyway.

'This system means that you have to keep records and you have to be organised about allowing time for review. But it's very popular with students. They would keep going on the mega-review for a whole lesson if I didn't stop them! It helps students to measure their progress. Especially at higher levels when they feel they've plateaued. They can *see* how much they've learned. They have to be encouraged, of course, to keep their own records too. I deal with that at the start of term, suggesting that they record words – not in bilingual lists, but like this:

The language item	A sentence in English	Information e.g. N., Vb.	Notes in own language

'That's so that they don't just rely on my record-keeping and my review sheets!

'I don't do the reviews and mega-reviews absolutely every week. If I'm bored with it or they're bored with it, we skip it. You can see by people's faces when they've had enough of it. But in feedback the students always say, "We liked the review times".'

(Mike Harding, a teacher of fourteen years' experience)

Students generally do like review and many teachers have it as a band running through many lessons in their timetables. The threads in this chapter are designed to fall within that band and to foster systematic review.

5.1

LEVEL
Lower elementary
– Intermediate,
with Advanced
variations

TIME
To introduce the
thread: 5 minutes
or less

MATERIALS
Sheets of poster
paper (or
wallpaper,
reversed);
something to fix
posters to the wall
with; access to a
(photo) copier

FOCUS
For students
Gradually building
up knowledge of
the meaning,
spelling and pro-
nunciation of
vocabulary;
encouraging the
habit of listening
for the stress
profiles of
vocabulary items
and making notes
about them

For you
Building a record
of the vocabulary
done with a
particular class;
reminding you to
indicate stress
and rhythm in a
non-auditory
mode

STRESS POSTERS/VOCABULARY POSTERS

Preparation

1 Stick to the wall or board one poster for each word stress pattern that you expect to occur among the words your students have met so far or are likely to meet that lesson.
2 At the top of each of your posters draw bold symbols for the appropriate stress patterns. For example, 'Oo' for *water* at the top of one poster, 'oO' for *hotel* on another, then 'OO' for *car key*, 'oOo' for *banana* and so on.
3 Think of a word to exemplify each pattern. These 'head' words should all be well known to your class and should contain no sounds that anyone has trouble with.

Introducing the thread (at elementary level)

1 Point to the symbols at the head of one poster. Say the head word for that pattern (e.g. *banana*) while highlighting its stress pattern in some way (e.g. by tapping out the rhythm of the syllables). Get your students to imitate your pronunciation.
2 Write this word at the top of what will become a column of words on that poster. Repeat with each of the other posters.
3 Tell your students that the name of each poster comes from the name of the first word on it, the 'head' word. Thus, they can call the posters 'the "banana" poster', 'the "water" poster' and so on. If you prefer, you can write each poster in a different colour, so students can refer to 'the red poster', 'the blue poster' and so on.
4 Every time a new word comes up, orally or gesturally highlight its stress pattern and ask your class which poster it should be on. When you get a correct answer, ask a student to write the word on the appropriate poster.

   Add more posters for different word stress patterns as they come up. (If you can't leave your posters stuck up on the walls, keep them all in a cardboard tube bearing the class name on the outside.)

From lesson to lesson

→ To review proper stressing of vocabulary on the posters, pair students up so that only one student in each pair can see the posters (or so that one student can see one half of the posters and the other student can see the other half). Student A tries to recall as many words as possible from an unseen poster. Student B corrects pronunciation, says if any words have been attributed to the wrong poster and, in the end, tells A which words on the poster A forgot.
→ Alternatively, Student A says a word from one poster and Student B says which poster he/she (B) thinks it's on.

→ Take one or more posters down. Replace each with a blank one. Hand out markers to one and all. Give the class five minutes to reconstruct the poster(s).

→ *Intermediate and advanced level:* These students may have more trouble with phrase stress than with word stress, e.g. stress in compound noun phrases (e.g. *trade union movement*) and verb+noun phrases (e.g. *racing car driver*). At this level, then, posters should focus only on areas of stress that are still difficult for some or all of the class.

ERROR CORRECTION

→ Point to the appropriate stress poster whenever you wish to indicate to a student that they have got the stress of a certain word or phrase wrong. Develop the system by encouraging other students to correct each other in this fashion.

→ If a student says a word with the wrong syllable stressed (e.g. *ho*tel), ask them which poster their pronunciation fits. If they pick the right poster for that stressing (e.g. the '*wa*ter' poster), say something like 'Yes, you have a good ear, but actually you need to say the word differently so that we can put it on a different poster. Which one, do you think?' Elicit help from other students if necessary.

HOMEWORK

If your students have a short text to read, ask them to use their dictionaries to find out which poster they would put each new bit of vocabulary on.

QUIZZING/TESTING

Take the posters down or conceal them and ask students to:

→ remember a certain number of items from each poster

→ fill in blank spots on a copy of the poster

→ sort out lexis taken from posters which you give them all jumbled up on a quiz sheet.

NEW LANGUAGE

Once the sense of the categorisation represented by the posters is clear, you can economically deal with the stress of a new item by simply associating it with a poster. Get students to say which poster they think the new item belongs on.

FILLER ACTIVITIES

Word stress posters can provide both early- and late-comers with useful work. Ask early-birds to think of a word or two that can be added to each poster. They check their ideas with you then write the words up. Late-comers can do the same thing while waiting for those who came on time to finish whatever they're in the middle of.

BORROWING FROM THE FRAMEWORK

Some students may begin to use elements of the stress poster system in their own notebooks. They may borrow or adapt your stress marking or they may apply the idea of categorisation to other elements of language (see the first variation below).

VARIATIONS

- Words can be grouped by topic rather than stress (see Animals word chart on p. 67), word class (i.e. nouns, verbs, etc.), register (e.g., formal, informal, neutral), place (as in the table below) or by some other principle.

One way of associating vocabulary with place

Shop	chemist's	newsagent's	florist's	baker's
What you can buy	aspirin	magazines	rose	sticky buns

- A particularly interesting variation is 'total word posters'. Here, when a new word comes up students vote on whether they want to learn it for recognition or production, or whether they don't think it's worth remembering at all.

1 If a 60 per cent majority decide for production, write the word on the poster in, say, red; otherwise use green for 'recognition'. Make it clear that the red words are ones that everyone must learn, including the lower-proficiency students, but that higher-proficiency students should try to learn some or all of the green words for production too.

   Add other information onto the poster near each word, e.g. one or two common collocations and register (abbreviate, e.g. n=neutral, f=formal, i=informal), positive or negative connotation (+ or –), word class and so on.

2 Once about twenty words have been noted in this way, conduct a review activity of some sort, e.g. a quiz.

3 Bearing in mind how students did in the review or quiz, strike out all the words which everyone has learned. Circle the ones learned by the fewest people.

4 After a couple more brief review activities, assign a student the job of redoing the poster with all the learned words omitted. This will create room for new words.

- Give each student or pair of students a poster to look after. Their job, both in class and out, is to keep their eyes and ears open for words that could go on their poster. When they have noted something down, they can add it to their poster. (Perhaps ask lower-level students to show you their notes beforehand on what they plan to add.) Either periodically allow class time for these additions and/or allow students to take their posters home with them. (This variation applies to other poster ideas too.)

CLASSROOM DICTIONARY

Although highly adaptable for use in preparation for a major exam, *Classroom dictionary* can play a broad, ongoing role in vocabulary learning throughout the time a group of language students remain together. Among other advantages, it results in a sizeable body of notes on what has been covered which can, for example, be copied for students who join a course late, or shown to a substituting teacher.

Preparation

Think of fifteen to thirty categories within each of which your class has learned a dozen or more words. At beginner level these categories will be very broad (e.g. 'activities') and it will be possible to encompass a high proportion of all the words your students actually know. At advanced level, categories will be much narrower (e.g. 'physical barriers': *wall, fence, hedge, railing, paling*) and will include a far smaller proportion of their total vocabularies.

Introducing the thread (at elementary level)

1   Take into a class as many sheets of A4 paper as you have students. Assign each student a different heading for them to write at the top of their sheet. At elementary level, for example, one student writes 'food' and another 'drink'. Other headings could be: 'colours', 'numbers', 'household objects', 'days and months', 'jobs', 'buildings', 'places to go', 'languages', 'actions', 'furniture', 'appliances'. *Note:* If you have a class larger than thirty, ask students to work in pairs.
2   Elicit a good example for each sheet. The student who has that sheet writes this example down. Make sure people don't write too big.
3   Set a time limit (e.g. two minutes) and ask everyone to add more words to their sheet. Remind them not to put words on their sheet that do not go with the heading. Ask them first of all to try to add words from memory but encourage them to look in their notes when their recollection flags. Allow mono- and bilingual dictionaries too for checking, but stress that students must write down *known* words and not wholly new ones.
      It is a good idea for you to begin to fill in a sheet too.
4   Call time. Explain that now the sheets are going to move around the class one place to the right. Once this is done, ask people to check the sheet that's been passed to them. They correct spelling errors and cross out vocabulary that doesn't fit the heading on the sheet. You do this, too, with the sheet that's been handed to you. Then people try to add more words to this, their new sheet. Again allow a couple of minutes. Then call time and ask people to change papers one place to the right again. Make sure everyone does it at the same time. From now on *you* don't add any words onto the

5.2

LEVEL
Any

TIME
15–80 minutes in the first lesson, depending on class size and variation

MATERIALS
A class set of blank sheets of A4 paper

FOCUS
Developing the habit of reviewing; experiencing a way of organising vocabulary notes by theme

sheet that comes to you but divide your time between quickly checking the sheet that comes to you and then circulating around the class to help students with spelling and so on.

5 When the sheets have circulated back to the students they started with, collect them in if you think you haven't been able to ensure that everything is spelled correctly. It may be possible to go through them all quickly on the spot and hand them back straight-away. Otherwise, hand them back, corrected, in the following lesson or, better still, ask students to go home and check one paper each using a dictionary.

6 Give each student the job of producing a fair copy of their sheet. Collect these in a following lesson. Run off a class set of (photo)copies of each in order to produce a complete classroom dictionary for each student in the class.

From lesson to lesson

→ Put each student in charge of a page in the classroom dictionary. Their job is to keep a record of newly learned vocabulary that belongs on that page. Periodically, organise a session during which these notes of new words are shared in class.

→ From time to time, encourage students to discuss whether any new pages are needed. For as your students' vocabularies grow in size, page headings need to become narrower in scope. If you have been working with a class for some time and the 'food' section in their dictionary is too large and disorganised, it will need to be rewritten on (for example) five separate sheets, one headed 'flavourings, herbs and spices' and others headed 'fruit', 'vegetables', 'cereals and cereal products' (e.g. wheat, pasta, bread, flour), 'high-protein foods' (e.g. beef, fish, eggs, cheese), and 'dishes made from various things' (e.g. pizza, hamburger).

→ Breaking down overgrown categories can be done in class or for homework by individuals. Check their sheets before the individ-ual students make their fair copies. Then run off class sets as before.

→ Vocabulary on one page can be further sub-divided, for example, students write vegetable names under sub-headings like 'green', 'yellow/orange' or, instead, class them by shape like this, 'leafy', 'roundish', 'long and roundish', or whatever.

→ Similarly, you can ask students to make pages for completely new sections. For example, lower intermediate students could add pages for such new categories as: 'prepositions' (with a brief example of each main meaning and, if possible, a diagram, e.g. 'look towards Mecca→●'); conjunctions (with an example for each); phrasal verbs; exponents for inviting (e.g. How about . . . ing?, Would you like to X?) and so on.

Naturally, if you have a new advanced class, you will not insist they start at the bottom by writing sections for broad categories like 'food' and 'animals'. Instead, try ones like 'types of government', 'adjectives of texture', 'currently fashionable clichés (e.g., *at the end of the day*) and so on.

VARIATIONS

1 Words can be grouped according to collocation, for example, one poster might be headed 'Make . . .' with items like *a cake, a good impression (on)* while others might be headed Do . . .', 'Take . . .', 'Have . . .', 'Get . . .' 'Turn . . .', 'Come . . .', 'Go . . .' and so on.

2 Make a dictionary on one topic, such as food, with each page relating to the topic in a different way (e.g. a page on raw foods, another on cooked foods, ways of cooking, foods with natural 'cases', i.e. foods with shells, peels, rinds, etc.), eating and cooking utensils, kitchen fixtures and appliances and so on. Take a broad topic, for example, 'animals', but add detail under extra headings (see chart below).

Animals word chart

Animal	horse	dog	cat
Female	mare	bitch	queen
Male	stallion, gelding	dog	tom
Young	foal, filly, colt, yearling	puppy	kitten
Breeds	Arab, shire, thoroughbred, . . .	spaniel, mongrel, . . .	Persian, tabby, 57 varieties, . . .
Colours	bay, chestnut, grey, pinto, palomino	brown, . . .	tabby, ginger, tortoiseshell
Hair	coat, mane, tail, feathers	fur, whiskers, hackles	fur, whiskers
'House'	stable	dog house, kennel	cat basket, cattery
Connected equipment	saddle, bridle, shoes, . . .	collar, lead	flea collar

To take another example, a poster on 'the law' could have vocabulary arranged under headings like 'the players' (judges, solicitors, . . .), 'places' (Magistrates' Court, Crown Court, remand centre, the dock . . .), 'types of law' (criminal, civil, marine, common . . .), 'sacred cows' (the right to silence, wigs, . . .), 'interesting sayings' ('He who represents himself has a fool for a client', . . .).

RATIONALE

- Beginner and elementary students really like the basic activity. They can consolidate word learning in a low-stress, non-test-like manner.
- The dictionary, being a group product, is evidence that cooperative work can have valuable results.
- The process of repeatedly adding to the dictionary and periodically reorganising it can serve as an example of the importance of accumulation, structuring, review and restructuring in other areas of language learning.
- *Classroom dictionary* can introduce students to important elements in keeping a notebook (e.g. quantity *plus* organisation, also periodic review).
- The activity can be very useful just before a test.
- It is good discipline for you, too, to keep track of what's come up.

5.3

LEVEL
Elementary+

TIME
5 minutes

FOCUS
Review; fluency
practice; fun

JUST A MINUTE

Introducing the thread (at elementary level)

A student speaks to the class for half a minute on a topic that the class has discussed before. For every correct use of a noun, verb or adjective connected with that topic, the speaker gets one point. If they pronounce it correctly, they get another point. Speakers can represent teams or not.

From lesson to lesson

→ *Intermediate level:* Divide the class into at least two teams. The activity begins with a representative of one team speaking. The time limit is one minute. Members of the other team should challenge the speaker every time they hear a mistake in one or two stipulated categories (e.g. word endings, word order, pronunciation, word stress, too much hesitation, etc.). When someone challenges, pause the time-keeping. When you have adjudicated the challenge, time-keeping resumes.

  Teams get ten points if a speaker speaks out the minute with no successful challenges; and five points if the speaker speaks out the whole minute, albeit with successful challenges. The opposing team gets one point for a correct challenge and an additional point if they can suggest a correct correction.

→ *Advanced level:* The rules are the same as for the intermediate level except that the person who makes a successful challenge takes over the role of speaker and tries to finish what remains of the minute. A team gets one point for a successful challenge and five points if it is a member of their team who is speaking *when the minute runs out*.

→ Let groups decide what categories challenges can be in.

ACKNOWLEDGEMENT
This activity is based on a BBC Radio 4 panel game. (The 'advanced' version is most like the original.)

TEST YOUR NEIGHBOUR

Introducing the thread

1 Say that everyone must think up three test questions for a neighbour to answer, relating to material just covered. Add that the answers will be 'graded', though not officially! You won't make any record of how people do.
2 Ask the class to decide on a fair grading system.
3 Ask them to make a short list of rules for a fair and useful review test, e.g.:

- The test should ask about what has been covered in the class.
- The test should ask about things that are useful to know.
- The test should fit the testee.

Steps 2 and 3 should only be necessary the first time this thread is used, although on subsequent occasions it is a good idea to remind students of what they decided on the first time.

4 Students ask their partners their questions. Afterwards, they give grades to their neighbours. Meanwhile, testees grade their partner's test questions in accordance with the rules agreed on in Step 3.

VARIATION
In the lesson before, tell lower-level students what the topic will be so they can prepare.

COMMENT
To underscore that you do not mean to get students involved in grading each other for real, create a background of humour. For example, warn that there will be a silly penalty for the worst test question, for example, standing up and walking twice around one's own chair.

5.4

LEVEL
Elementary+

TIME
5 minutes+

MATERIALS
None

FOCUS
Review

5.5

LEVEL
Elementary

TIME
5–10 minutes

MATERIALS
None

FOCUS
Review

SELECTIVE REMEMBERING

Introducing the thread

1 Specify a certain, more or less recent, period of class time, for example: 'the last half hour', 'the lesson before this one', 'the lessons this week', 'the activity yesterday where we did X'.

2 Ask students to think back to that period and remember vocabulary items in one or two of the following categories. They should make notes on items they think:

- are important to remember for school
- are important to remember for real life
- they knew before but had forgotten.
  And on ones which:
- they are afraid they might forget
- remind them of something not directly connected with the meaning of the word
- are ugly or appealing in some way or are totally emotionally neutral to them
- they think someone else in the class should learn (ask them to note down the names).

EXTENSION

3 In pairs or groups, students compare and discuss which items they've noted down.

4 Ask everyone to report one thing a partner noted down and why.

From lesson to lesson

→ Add new review categories.

→ Read out a menu of 'review categories'. Students write down the one(s) they find interesting and then review accordingly.

→ Students suggest review categories.

COMMENT

In all the other review threads in this chapter, low- and high-proficiency students will tend to remember different amounts of vocabulary (functional exponents, verb forms, etc.). In *Selective remembering*, however, what is remembered or reviewed is not just determined by proficiency but by interest as well.

ACKNOWLEDGEMENT
We learned the idea of putting words into affective categories from Morgan and Rinvolucri (1986).

MAPPING

This thread focuses on more than just recall. It gives students the opportunity to gain insights into the broader relationships among items and information met in previous lessons.

LEVEL
Elementary+

TIME
15–90 minutes or even more, depending on the period of time being reviewed

Introducing the thread

1 Ask students to produce an overview of what they've encountered or learned over a certain period of time, e.g. that day's lesson, a recent lesson, a day or a series of lessons. Ask students if they want to work in pairs, small groups or as a whole class.

2 First they recall things, usually fairly haphazardly. Then they begin to organise the material they've recalled. This will stimulate questions to neighbours, to you, to the whole group.

MATERIALS
None

FOCUS
Global review

Some of the ways in which students can organise their mappings are as follows:

- In answer to the question, 'What did we do?', students write down a chronology of activities, events and information in, as far as they can, the order in which these things were experienced or encountered. The chronology can run from first to last or from last to first.
- Students recall and ponder in response to a question such as, 'What have we learned about X?' (e.g. about religion in Britain, about formal v informal English, about ways of talking about the future).
- They make lists of key words for the period stipulated.
- They try to reproduce the drawings, diagrams, time lines, boardwork they encountered during this period.
- They try to recall and list all the situations, places or people referred to. And so on.
- They can make 'route maps' (see Fig. 14) instead of lists, or use any other layout of prompts and information they like.

RATIONALE
- Students need encouragement to bring disparate recollections together into a coherent whole which makes sense to them.
- The process of making the representations (1) may help students to see what they know and what they haven't understood or have forgotten, and (2) may help them to see a whole where before they saw only disparate facts and experiences.
- Visual representations of this whole may enhance recall.

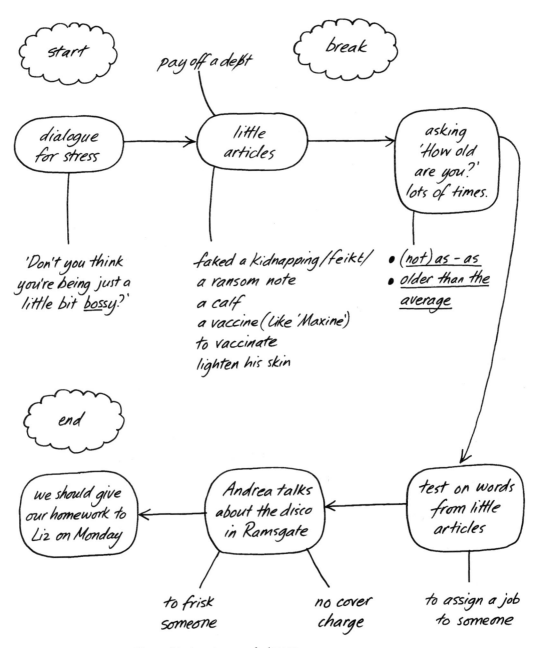

Figure 14 A route map of a lesson.

CHAPTER 6

Short pieces of writing

It is important to provide learners of all levels with regular *small-scale* writing practice.

i   Short pieces of writing are less daunting for the student and so more likely to be completed.

ii They are easier to include in class time than longer ones.

- One advantage here is that there are some teaching/learning situations where students are unlikely to do written work unless they do it in class (e.g. some unassessed ESL and EFL courses, especially if students are working during the course or are on holiday).
- Another advantage is that it is easier for students to consult you *while* they are writing. This makes it more likely that they will be able to express themselves accurately and, from this, gain in confidence.
- As you may often be able to read and comment on finished work on the spot or during a break, students get quicker feedback than on longer pieces of writing.
- You can integrate short pieces of writing into other course work much more effectively.

iii Sentence-length and paragraph-length written work typically provides sufficient evidence for diagnosis of the kinds of things students need to work on, e.g. knowledge about conventions of capitalisation, punctuation and layout; control of grammar; aptness of word choice; ability to link thoughts comprehensibly; common discourse patterns and so on. In important respects, longer assignments often amount to overkill, being far longer than they need to be in order to afford necessary practice and feedback.

Interestingly, Cohen (1987) suggests that a good deal of the written feedback students get on returned writing assignments is either not even read by them or is poorly understood, partly because of some teachers' habit of making vague or confusing margin comments like 'vague or 'confusing'. Giving shorter assignments makes it easier for you, either face to face or in margin notes, to express your thoughts about student successes and errors in a full, intelligible and more conversational form. For example, 'There is something I don't quite understand here. Do you mean . . . or . . .?' (Explain to students that you can give them better feedback if they leave an extra wide margin either at the left or right of each of their sheets.) In any case, students are also more likely to notice and remember errors, corrections and comments if these are few, rather than numerous as is more likely in the case of long pieces of writing.

iv If students have got a short assignment wrong in some important respect (e.g. they have written about the wrong topic or have got a recurring verb form wrong), they are less likely to get deeply frustrated than if they have made similar mistakes in a long assignment.

v Short writing tasks allow students to do a little bit of writing and then get feedback. This is bound to be preferable to their spending a considerable time on a longer stretch of writing and possibly making the same kind of mistake over and over again before getting feedback.

vi There can be more variety in topic.

vii You avoid the horror of getting dozens of multi-page homeworks all at once.

viii Giving short written assignments means that 'writing' can be a band running from lesson to lesson. Concentrating on writing long texts at (and at lower elementary level even ten lines can be a very long text) typically means that writing has to be planned as an occasional block taking up most or all of a lesson.

With a fairly homogeneous class, you can gradually introduce Threads 6.1–6.5 in the order given. When introducing a new thread, though, you need not drop the previous one. That is, whether you decide in a given lesson to ask students to write paragraphs (Thread 6.4) or join sentences (Thread 6.2) will depend on what other work you're doing at the moment. With a heterogeneous class, you can proceed similarly, but may often decide to have less proficient students work with earlier threads and more proficient students with later ones. Or, when using the same thread with everyone, you can give different students more or less challenging versions of it. For example, if using thread 6.2, *Joining sentences*, ask more proficient students to work with conjunctions which your less proficient students have not encountered yet. However, most of these threads are inherently open-ended, that is, they allow students to challenge themselves to a degree suited to their level of English.

SENTENCES

Introducing the thread

6.1

LEVEL
Elementary –
Upper
intermediate

MATERIALS
None

TIME
5 minutes+

FOCUS
Writing
sentences;
personalisation of
a set topic

1 Either after or some time during each of the next six lessons, ask students to write one sentence. Set the topics, e.g.:
   - the senses: something you see/hear/touch/taste/smell every day
   - the tenses: something you do every day/did yesterday/are going to do tomorrow/have never done/had done before you got to school yesterday.
2 Take the sentences in and correct them 'positively' (see Fig. 18). Respond to each with a full sentence of your own. See Figure 18 for an example of this.

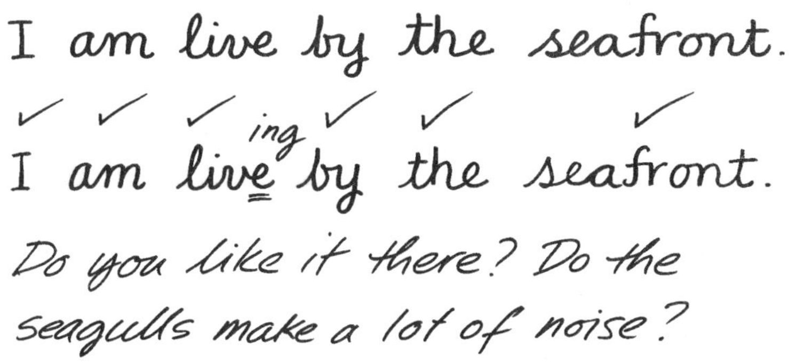

> I am live by the seafront.
>
> ✓ ✓ ✓ _ing_ ✓ ✓   ✓
> I am live by the seafront.
>
> Do you like it there? Do the
> seagulls make a lot of noise?

Figure 18

original
corrected
teacher response

VARIATIONS

Instead of specifying a theme, specify a number of words. Aside from doing that, say only that the sentences must be true. Interestingly, students tend to find the highly arbitrary structure of a low word limit a stimulus to creativity. Writings of this sort surprisingly often convey information students really want you to know. Here are three such messages we've received lately:

I didn't like to write before.
We all had a late party last night.
My landlady makes me pay for baths.

RATIONALE

Responding to the sentences confirms to students that their sentences have a purpose, that they are not just writing for writing's sake but that the ideas they express have independent importance. For more on response and reformulation with student writing see Peyton and Staton 1991.

6.2

LEVEL
Elementary+,
especially EAP
(English for
Academic
Purposes)

TIME
10 minutes+

FOCUS
Using single and
multi-word
connectors

JOINING SENTENCES

Introducing the thread

Over a series of lessons, focus on a group of similar connectors. Ask students to write two separate sentences. They then link the ideas in these two sentences by writing a third sentence using a connector or connectors. Give a different connector, or joining word/phrase, each day. Choose from, e.g.:

and:
as well as, too
also, additionally, in addition
plus, moreover, furthermore

either . . . or

but:
yet, still, however, although, even so, nevertheless
whereas
alternatively
on the one hand . . . on the other, but then again, some people say . . . but others feel . . .

anyway:
anyhow, at any rate

on the contrary

because:
for the reason that, owing/due to the fact that

so:
therefore, consequently, accordingly, hence, as a result, thus

if:
unless
provided that, in case, as long as

actually:
in fact

for . . . to

to:
in order to, so that, so as to

Thus, to practise *and* elementary students could write:

I like ice cream. I like apples. I like ice cream and apples.

Intermediate students could come up with:

I like ice cream. I also like apples.

Advanced students could produce:

I like ice cream. I'm very partial to apples as well!

Advanced students can of course also work with more complex categories of connectors, such as *for . . . to.*

To practise *for . . . to* upper intermediate/advanced students could write:

He called an election. That was stupid. For him to call an election was stupid.

From lesson to lesson

→ When introducing a connector, associate it with a symbol. Thus, we associate:

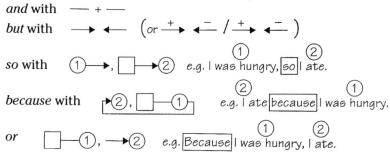

→ As you introduce a new connector, it is sometimes possible to associate it with a symbol that has already been introduced. Thus, *therefore* can be associated with the symbol for *so*. Often though, as you focus on a new connector, you may need to vary your symbols somewhat. Thus, at first *but* can be ⟶ ⟵ . But when you introduce *although*, you may want to represent *but* like this: ⟶.☐◄⟵ or ⟶,☐◄⟵ and *although* like this: ☐⊢⟶,◄⟵ or ⟶ ☐◄⟵. .

(The box indicates the position of the connector.) But retain the original symbol ⟶ ⟵ as a blanket symbol for all such 'adversative' connectors, — + — for all 'additive' connectors and so on.

→ Some connectors can be represented somewhat more pictorially (see Fig. 19).

Figure 19 *on the one hand . . . on the other*

→ Ask students to group connectors in their notebooks under the blanket symbols – & 'basic' connectors. Under each heading, students keep notes on the differences between the connectors grouped together there. For example:

- *therefore* under *so*; marked 'formal'
- *whereas* under *but*; with the notes 'connects sentences with different subjects'; 'emphatic; somewhat formal'
- *too* under *and*; with the note 'suggests that the last thing is more unexpected'.

Model sentences should be noted down as well, in order to suggest nuances of meaning and use and to show where in a sentence or set of sentences a given connector tends to occur and with what punctuation.

→ In higher-level classes, as you move beyond review of basic, everyday connectors (e.g. *and*, *but*, *so*, *also*) to ones like *therefore* and *thus*, teach a paraphrase along with your symbol. This should help your students develop a better understanding of how these items should be used. Crewe (1990) suggests a number of paraphrases, e.g.:

therefore, thus:
on account of this situation, because of these events, as a consequence of this
however, on the other hand:
in spite of this, a different view is, in opposition to this
on the contrary:
that this is untrue is shown by
further, in addition:
that is supported by, another consideration is
furthermore, moreover:
another (more) important point is, a decisive factor in this was
anyhow, anyway:
whichever way it is, whatever the reason is
actually, in fact:
it has to be admitted that

W J Crewe, 'The illogic of logical connectives'

→ Ask students to do more complex combinations, such as, *I like swimming and running. You already know I like reading. As well as reading, I like swimming and running.*

Note: Time order conjunctions (*before*, *after*, *first*, *next*) are not usually too troublesome, especially for higher-proficiency students.

RATIONALE/COMMENT

Even advanced students who recognise dozens of conjunctive devices may have a very scrambled notion of when to use many of them. That is one reason to be as careful as you can in teaching their meaning/use. A different flaw in the writing of many higher-level learners is that they overstuff their prose with connectors. Make sure you don't leave students with the impression that using lots of connectors is a necessary hallmark of clear writing. It isn't. Think carefully before saying that any two connectors are completely synonymous. This is far less often the case than some writers suggest. See Crewe (1990) for much common sense and some good tips in this area.

SEVERAL SENTENCES

Introducing the thread (at elementary/intermediate level)

Ask students to write several sentences on the same topic. Give them some structural and/or content guidelines, e.g.:

- Describe an event. Use: *First . . ., And then, . . ., A bit later on, . . ., Next, . . .*
- Describe a person. Use: *She's . . . with . . . and . . ., She usually wears . . .*
- Describe a place. Use: *There's a / There're some . . ., It's . . ., It's got . . .*
- Describe an object. Give: size, shape, texture, colour, use. Use: *It is . . ., It's for -ing . . .*
- Describe a procedure. For example, use: *First . . ., Then . . ., Next . . .*

Depending on what is to be described, students make predominant use of:

→ *you* plus the active voice where a personal tone is appropriate (especially in instructions for procedures likely to be carried out by the addressee, e.g. *First you put the plug in and then turn on the taps*)

→ *they* plus the active voice (especially in describing procedures not expected to be carried out by the addressee, e.g. *They pick the hops in the autumn . . .*)

→ the passive voice where a personal tone is inappropriate (especially in describing industrial procedures)

→ verbal nouns (especially in a fairly formal style where compactness of expression is desired, e.g. *First comes harvesting, then washing and sorting, then packing, distribution to wholesalers and . . .*).

EXTENSION (TO LINK WITH THREAD 6.4)

Students form groups and collate their sentences on one topic to produce a more substantial description of:
- an event they have all witnessed or attended
- a person/group of people/class/family
- a country/town/place/ room full of objects
- an object
- a sequence of steps in a process, e.g. getting ready for a long trip.

6.3

LEVEL
Elementary+

TIME
10 minutes+

MATERIALS
None

FOCUS
Producing short, cohesive texts

From lesson to lesson

→ Writing 'mini-texts' is often popular with students and provides good freer practice in joining sentences. Set an *exact* word limit – 37 words, 50, whatever (between about 35 and 60 seems to work best) – and a minimum number of sentences, say three. Then, set a topic and/or give them a few words they must include in their text and/or specify a genre, e.g. plot outline, newspaper article and/or a discourse structure (e.g. general statement, perhaps about their country, followed by a specific example; or, background situation, then problem, then solution, then evaluation). Again, an arbitrary word limit tends to be amazingly effective as a spur to creativity. Perhaps everyone thinks, 'Well, 37 words, that's nothing. I can do that.' And 'writer's block' vanishes.

6.4

LEVEL
Elementary+

TIME
10 minutes+

MATERIALS
None

FOCUS
The form and organisational principles of the paragraph

PARAGRAPHS

Introducing the thread

1 Elicit or give the 'rules' of writing paragraphs and show examples for each of them.
  ● One paragraph, one main topic.
  ● The first line is indented, or a line is skipped between paragraphs.
  ● Write to the *end* of each line.
  ● Don't make sentences too long. (A dozen words or so is usually plenty.)
  ● Don't use too many conjunctions.
  ● Put sentences in some sort of order, for example, in time order.
  ● A paragraph may have a 'topic' (introductory) and/or a concluding sentence.
2 Ask for one short paragraph from each student, to be done as homework.
3 Depending on the type of group, type of lesson and so on, you can ask for paragraphs on different topics, e.g. any of the ones from Thread 6.3 *Several sentences*, or ones which:
  ● introduce/conclude an imaginary essay
  ● present cause(s) and effect(s)
  ● make a general statement or claim, and give examples or substantiation
  ● present the advantages and/or disadvantages of something
  ● compare X and Y
  ● are any combinations of the above that would build naturally, one by one, into an essay, article, short story or other format students are working towards.

EXTENSION

Students are more willing to redraft paragraphs than longer pieces of writing. Take advantage of this to give students experience of writing as a 'write and edit' process. (This applies to sub-paragraph length writings too.)

From lesson to lesson

→ Elicit sentences from students on a given topic. You or they write them up on the board. They order and integrate them to produce a paragraph. Higher-level students can work with skeleton sentences (e.g. *doctors in training / terrible workload*).

→ An enjoyable freer practice activity is 'Filling In A Shape'. Ask students to draw the outline of their home country (or that of a fish, flower, coffee cup, their house or the building their home is in, or whatever). The outline should be large enough to contain several sentences. Students write whatever they have to say about the topic suggested by the outline *inside* the outline. (They can curve their sentences to fit as necessary.)

RATIONALE

● The shape stimulates thoughts and gets students writing quickly.

● The shape is a visual clue as to what a good topic sentence ought to relate to.

● If the shapes are drawn small enough to accommodate a few sentences only, even lower-level students will feel the challenge is one they can tackle.

LEARNER DIARIES

Introducing the thread (at beginner level)

Begin by asking students to keep one word records of lessons or lesson phases, e.g. *easy, difficult, fun, boring, useful*.

From lesson to lesson

→ Eventually they begin to write sentences. Prompt them by suggesting sentence heads, e.g.:

Today I	learned . . .
	understood . . .
	couldn't understand . . .
	we . . .
Yesterday	I . . .
	my neighbour . . .

6.5

LEVEL
Any

TIME
5 minutes+

MATERIALS
Each student needs a notebook

FOCUS
Free writing; reflection on one's own ways of learning and on particular learning experiences

→ Students write one paragraph a day. To encourage them to vary and extend their repertoires of language and topics, suggest additional sentence heads from time to time, e.g.:

We studied . . .	(content/material)
We did it by . . .	(process/activity)
I was happy with . . .	(personal progress)
I couldn't really get . . .	(personal progress)
My neighbour/group/classmates . . .	(personal/group relations)
I had just . . .	(chronology)
I was going to go on to . . .	(chronology)
I feel/felt . . .	(mood)
I like/dislike/suggest . . .	(attitude)
I wish I knew how to say . . .	(needs)
Things I want to remember . . .	(needs)

→ Negotiate a policy with students – individually or as a class – as to whether the diaries are read (or even corrected) and if so how, what for, how often, whether they are read out or read by others and whether diary writing is done in class.

→ Your perceptions of the class and the course can be sharpened if you join in the diary writing (see Murphey 1992).

→ See also the accounts of interactive dialogue journals in Peyton and Staton 1991.

CHAPTER 7

New ways of thinking, personal themes

In our teacher training we are taught what is significant and what is not. We thus learn to think and act in terms of certain categories, such as 'listening skills practice' and 'grammar practice'. This is one of the things that belonging to a professional community is all about. We have to make sure, however, that neither we nor our professional community are increasingly fossilised within a shrinking set of practices and conceptual frameworks. It's important we don't become clones of each other. In Chapter 4 and now again in this chapter there are some glimpses of less usual ways of categorising the stuff of teaching and learning, ways that you probably won't come across in other teacher's resource books or books on teacher training or teacher development. An individual teacher may think of a set of ideas to work on in class but then be held back by the thought 'Well, that's not really what I'm supposed to do. I'm supposed to do standard EFL things.' We would like that teacher to follow their instincts about what is significant in language classes as long as the lessons that result are useful and interesting to students.

7.1

LEVEL
Lower
intermediate+

TIME
5–90 minutes or
longer

MATERIALS
Variable

FOCUS
Encouraging
flexible and
innovative
thinking and
language use;
being playful;
practising
language in the
context of
intellectual
activities or of
everyday pieces
of knowledge that
are useful and
interesting in
their own right

STIMULUS-BASED TEACHING

Stimulus-based teaching is about using a stimulus either to build one whole lesson as a block or to start a thread which will extend over two or more lessons. You can:

- use all the stages of working described below in one lesson
- take one stimulus and use it over a period of time, gradually introducing the different stages
- take a different stimulus each time *and* use a different stage. The stimulus can be an object, a visit, a series of sounds, anything that stimulates!

Introducing the thread

The procedure divides into the following five stages which we will summarise before giving examples.

1 ENCOUNTERING THE STIMULUS
Typically, students first encounter the stimulus while it is hidden or obscured in some sense. For example, if the stimulus is a picture or a text you can:

- flash it to allow only a brief glimpse or two
- allow everyone to have a good long look but mask part of it
- mask it entirely and reveal (part of) it by sliding the masking away very slowly
- hand out the whole thing, but in pieces, with different people getting different bits.

Rationale: Not displaying all of the material immediately, or displaying it only for a short time, means that students can speculate, predict, describe, match, sort, recombine and reorder (see below). And, in performing these tasks, students can be learning and using useful language.

2 ANALYSIS
Once the stimulus is fully available to the students, the key options are as follows:

- Students comment on their reactions to the whole stimulus and compare these to their earlier speculations.
- Students identify and name parts or aspects of the stimulus. (If the stimulus is a text, this stage consists of reading/listening tasks designed to get students to notice language and understand content.)
- Students describe the stimulus.
- Students speculate about: what the stimulus is made of; how, when, why and where it was produced; by whom or what; ingredients, materials or design in the past, now, in the future; its natural context; its past, present and future states or uses; what it represents; where to get more information, etc.

For the Analysis stage, and the three that follow, what is said of the stimulus tends to apply *literally* if the stimulus is an object and *figuratively* if the stimulus is more or less intangible.

3 PERSONALISATION

This can include individual students speaking or writing about their personal experience of the stimulus; how it is similar or different from them; what they would do if . . .; mental associations evoked by the stimulus; quantifying elements of the stimulus; individual students speaking or writing about their personal experience (real or imaginary) of the stimulus. (See below for examples.)

4 ALTERATION AND TRANSFORMATION

Options here include students making new things from the components of the stimulus, reducing or expanding it, thinking of parallels or analogies, opposites or reversals.

Again, these activity names tend to have a more literal meaning in the case of physical objects and a more figurative meaning in the case of less physical stimuli. For example, if you ask students to say what the 'opposite' of an apple is, they may say, 'an apple turned inside out', 'a similarly-sized piece of outer space', 'a plastic apple', 'a zebra', 'an infinity of apples', 'a black apple' 'anything that isn't an apple' or 'an apple seed'. If you ask them to turn a text into its opposite, they may just add or remove negatives throughout or they may think of an opposite for each word in one or all of the ways just exemplified for *apple*. Or again, transforming a potato could mean decorating it or carving it so that it becomes a rudimentary stamp printer or a potato jack-o'-lantern. Transforming a text could mean changing all the general words (e.g. *say, hold, go*) into ones rich in image and connotation (e.g. *gush, clutch, flee*), or vice versa if you start with a passage from a popular romantic novel.

5 CREATION/EMPATHY

Here students move on beyond manipulation of the stimulus. This can mean, for example, creating a role play suggested in some way by the stimulus. If the stimulus is a button, the role play might involve someone trying to buy a single button in a shop which only sells sets of six sewn onto cards.

To review, the starting point of this type of lesson is simply anything that is sufficiently amusing or interesting to students, or which you can present in such an interesting way, that it:
- stimulates their curiosity
- provokes a response
- arouses a desire to find out more about the stimulus, to analyse and play with it.

Whether the stimulus is concrete or intangible, you can subject it to different movements and processes, either literally or figuratively.

You don't, of course, use all possible options in each stage each time you use a stimulus. You might not even want always to go through all five stages, as sometimes this would take too long or be too predictable. (One of the motives for planning lessons or threads around a stimulus might well be, just that, to be unpredictable and, thereby, cause students to participate with extra attention and interest.)

TIP

In addition to selecting some activities to do at one stage and rejecting others, you can interpret the same activity in different ways on different occasions. Take, for example, the idea of 'reducing the stimulus', usable in the 'Alteration/Transformation' stage. If applied to a short text, this basic idea yields such variations as:

* Reading the text aloud but at reduced volume. For example, students read sub-vocally.

Rationale: Everyone can practise at once without disturbing the others.

* 'Faster'n'faster': Here, the *time* taken to read the text aloud is reduced. Starting very slowly, students read an easy text, such as a short dialogue or anecdote, several times. Each time they read it faster. For the slowest reading ask students to read as if speaking over a very bad phone line; for faster readings, as if their time on a pay phone is about to run out.

Rationale: Fun and fluency.

(See Rinvolucri 1984, pp. 59–60 and 90–91 for two other highly interesting and useful text reduction activities.)

Here are two examples of how to implement the five stages.

First introduce vocabulary and structures as appropriate to your students' level.

EXAMPLE 1: USING AN APPLE AS THE STIMULUS

ENCOUNTERING THE STIMULUS

1 You have the apple thickly wrapped with newspaper in a bag.
2 Write some sentence starters on the board:

I think . . .,
It's . . ., definitely
It's probably . . .
It could be . . .
It can't be . . .

3 Students feel the apple through the bag and speculate about what the object is and use the language above to do so.
4 Elicit a word for its shape. Ask for more shape words. Write them on the board.
5 Elicit a word for its texture. Ask for more texture words. Write them on the board.
6 Keeping the apple in the bag, remove the wrapping of newspaper.

Let students feel again. Write the following sentence on the board,

If it was a . . ., it'd be . . . -er

7 Students make sentences like this:

If it was a potato, it'd be a bit longer.
If it was a grapefruit, it'd be bigger.
If it was a kiwi fruit, it'd be smaller/rougher/fuzzy.

ANALYSIS
1 Take the apple out of the bag and set it where everyone can see it.
2 Elicit or teach names for its parts (*peel, stem, core, flesh, pips*, etc.).
   Produce a labelled poster.
3 Ask how apples 'happen' and where they come from.
   Nouns: *apple tree, blossom, pollen, bees*
   Verbs: *grow, pollinate, pick*
   Time expressions: *in the beginning, then*
   Ask how apples get to our homes.
   Structures: *People/They* (verb) *them* or, *The apples/They are*
   (verb)*ed*
   Verbs: *pick, put, load, transport*
   Nouns: *buckets, boxes, lorries, storage shed*
4 Everyone gets an apple and examines it carefully.
   Vocabulary: *stem, freckles, bruise, worm hole, red, yellow, waxy, dull,*
   shiny, blotchy

PERSONALISATION
Each student writes at least three sentences saying what they and
their apple have in common, and at least three saying how they and
it differ. Students then share their sentences in pairs or groups.

ALTERATION/TRANSFORMATION
This can be literal, for example:
1 In a one-to-one class you and your student each pare off the peel of
   your apple in one long strip. Both of you toss the whole peel over
   your right shoulder onto the floor behind. Say: 'What letter of the
   alphabet does the shape of the peel most resemble? That's the first
   letter of the name of your future husband/wife/first child.' (or whatever seems appropriate).
2 Then elicit or teach vocabulary for the steps of eating (e.g. *take a
   bite, chew, taste/savour, swallow*) adding, for fun, 'optional ones'
   (e.g. *burp, choke*). Then, call out the steps and everyone begins to
   eat their apple.
Or the alteration can be figurative, e.g.:
   i   Everyone closes their eyes.
   ii Ask them to picture their apples in their mind's eye.
   iii Lead a guided visualisation by asking them to imagine it with
       yellow and blue stripes, covered in fur, gigantic with themselves
       sitting on top if it, etc.

CREATION/EMPATHY

Give students writing or speaking tasks as follows: 'Suppose the apple told its life story, what would it say? What would it say were the high and low points of its life?' Or: 'What do the pips feel? Are they comfortable? What plans do they have?'

EXAMPLE 2 USING TWO LINES OF TEXT AS THE STIMULUS

ENCOUNTERING THE STIMULUS

a Tell students the title of the two-line text. They guess the topic, content or what will be in it.
Or:
b Whisper one or two (consecutive) words from the text to each student. (Add words to your text to make enough to go around, or, conversely, omit some.) Students order themselves or their words to make a two-line text. Conduct them in a rapid recitation of the text, each student saying only their own word(s). If two adjacent students have different parts of a natural contraction, try to get them to contract the words as naturally as they can (e.g. a student with *will* says 'wo' and a student with *not* says 'n't'). Good fun!

ANALYSIS

1 Present the whole text.
2 Elicit first reactions, e.g. *I thought it would be about* . . .
3 Ask where it could have come from, e.g. *It looks like a little bit out of a newspaper/short story/advert* . . .
4 Ask: 'What does it mean?', 'What do its parts mean?' 'What are the names of all its parts?' ('Subject, verb, complement, object, etc.', or 'noun, verb, quantifier etc.', or 'word, capital letter, lower-case letter, space, line space, comma, full stop, etc.'.)

PERSONALISATION

Suppose the text contains the phrase 'a short way from the village':
1 Ask everyone to quantify *short* in this context. That is, students each write down a measurement (e.g. 'five minutes' walk', 'ten minutes by car', '500 metres') and then compare and explain why they think their measure of distance is short.
2 Ask, 'If you lived there, how would you cover this distance and why?'

ALTERATION/TRANSFORMATION

Students do one or more of the following:
a Pick a longish word out of the text and make as many smaller words from it as they can.
b Think of the opposite of three nouns or verbs (cf. the 'apple' example on p. 87). Students then read out their altered texts to each other.
c Reduce it (cf. p. 87).

d Expand it by adding in other words or adding sentences to the beginning or end.

e Substitute a new noun for each noun, a new verb for each verb and so on, while aiming to produce texts that have a sense they can explain. Students exchange their new texts.

CREATION/EMPATHY

Some options here are:

a If the text mentions an office but not, for instance, a rug, then say there's a rug in the office. Ask what size, colour, pattern, shape it is, what marks are on it, what other rug does it remind them of, where was it bought, who bought it for whom, etc. (see Stevick 1986 for this and other ideas on student-formed images).

b Conduct a guided visualisation by posing a chain of leading statements and questions, slowly and gently, with lots of time in between, e.g.: 'This office, there's a picture on one wall. Which wall? Does this wall catch the sun? At what time of day? The picture has a frame. What does it look like? There's a person in the picture. How old are they? This person is wearing something really bright. What is it?' While you're asking these questions, the students are building mental pictures. Afterwards, students write or tell others what they saw.

c Say: 'It's dusk. You are a window pane in the office. From the inside, you're a bit like a mirror. What are you reflecting?'

From lesson to lesson

Use different activities in the different stages. The five broad stages can form headings under which you can collect and store teaching ideas. Keep a notebook with a long section of blank pages for each of the five stages. Whenever you encounter a teaching activity or technique you like, write its name and its steps in an appropriate section. Again, these five stages can be applied to absolutely *any* stimulus.

7.2

LEVEL
Elementary+

TIME
3–8 minutes

MATERIALS
None

FOCUS
Building up stocks of concrete nouns, adjectives and words for describing shapes

THINGS OF THIS SHAPE

Introducing the thread

1 Draw a series of numbered circles on the board (see Fig. 20). The smallest circle should be barely visible from where the students are sitting. The largest should be as big as the board will accommodate. Add two or three numbers for circles too big to draw on the board, but which you indicate by gesture or by calling out a measurement. (The circles can stand for discs or spheres.)

2 On a sheet of paper, each student writes down the numbers of the circles, and by each number they write the word for a roundish thing that is the size of the circle in question. They cannot, though, use adjectives of size like *big* or *little*. Thus, for Circle 2, they can write *pea* but not *very little apple*.

3 Students go to the board and write their words near (or in) the appropriate circles. Thus, for Figure 20, you might have words such as *pea, mothball, golf ball, apple, grapefruit, globe of the world, boulder, the moon.*

From lesson to lesson

→ Draw different shapes, for example, square planes (*postage stamp→cornfield*), rectangular planes (*cigarette paper→ Manitoba*), cubes (*sugar cube→block of flats*), cylinders (*toothpick→ the Channel Tunnel*), cones (*golf tee→Mount Fuji*), three-dimensional ovals (*peanut→submarine*)

→ Repeat a shape but add additional sizes. In higher-level classes, elicit more objects for each size and more objects of different sizes.

→ Encourage the use of bilingual dictionaries.

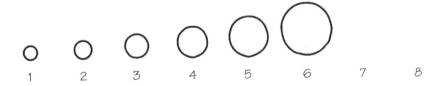

Figure 20

SCALES AND STEPS

Preparation

1 Consider the lexis you think your students know already or should be taught during your course.

2 Decide which items fall into narrow thematic or notional sets like 'adjectives applicable to air temperature' (e.g. *hot, warm, cool, cold, freezing*), 'distance between two things' (e.g. *far away from, distant from, near to, right by, against*) and so on.

3 Now rank these words by intensity along bipolar scales like the items in the two sets mentioned in Step 2 (see Fig. 21).

4 Think about what words fit on each scale and what words don't.

  i Segregate words according to the topic they apply to. Test the words you think of (or which you find in a wordbook like the *Longman Activator* or a thesaurus) in a short sentence frame. For example, 'It's ——— today' will accommodate adjectives (e.g. *hot*) and adjectival verbs (e.g. *boiling*).

  ii Some words may well have crept in that don't really belong. They may, for example, relate to notions other than the one your scale is based on. For instance, *dank, humid* and *sultry* introduce the notion of the moisture content of the air. Simply to plonk them on the *hot–cold* scale would be misleading. When you get a largish group of such oddballs, see if they will fit on scales of their own or whether they are better placed around intersecting scales, as in Figure 22.

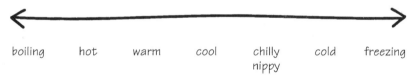

Figure 21 Sorting temperature words onto a scale

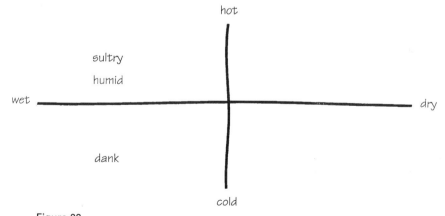

Figure 22

7.3

LEVEL
Elementary+

MATERIALS
Large board; student notebooks; (optional): sheets of poster paper (or wallpaper, reversed); something to fix posters to the wall with

FOCUS
For students
Recording vocabulary in a form that enhances recall and helps students to see at a glance how new lexis relates in meaning to familiar lexis and to see at a glance how much they have learned; giving them an idea (from the gaps in scales) how many words there may yet be to learn; understanding important types of relationships within particular word families, for example, among words that group along bipolar scales of magnitude or intensity, e.g. *small, big; shy, outgoing; hot, cold*

For you
Packing
information in
dense but
scannable form;
saving time that
might otherwise
be spent on less
efficient verbal
(rather than
visual) forms of
explanation;
diagnosing the
level of new
students and
assessing the
effectiveness of
one's own
teaching; coping
with mixed-ability
classes

Introducing the thread (at elementary level)

1 Teach the basic, standard words for the extremes of your topic area. For weather temperature, for example, these are *hot* v *cold*.

2 On the board, draw a horizontal or vertical scale. Label a point near one end 'hot' and a point near the other end 'cold'.

3 As new words fitting on this scale are met in reading or listening texts, as students or you introduce them in the classroom, add them onto the scale either (a) between your basic words (as with *cool* and *warm*), or (b) beyond them (as with *freezing* and *boiling*). Ask students to draw these scales in a special section of their notebooks. Additionally, reproduce your scales on posters. (See *Variations* below.)

4 As new words come up you can often teach them with a minimum of fuss just by pointing to their location on the (proper) scale.

From lesson to lesson

→ Add new scales for:
- wholly new topic areas, e.g.: prices of objects (*cheap, reasonable, dear/expensive, pricy, exorbitant*), amount of water in the air (*misty, drizzling, raining, pouring*), sociableness of people (*shy, outgoing*). Don't forget each time to provide a stem sentence such as 'She's a ——— person' or just 'She's ———'. Ask students to think of at least one exemplifying sentence for each new word which they can then write in their notebooks.
- related topic areas, e.g.: water temperature (*hot, cold*, etc. plus *tepid, lukewarm, scalding*).

→ Add new applications of known scales within an overall topic. For example, begin with adjectives for prices of food, then add applications to other things you can buy. Or start with the prices of food and then go on to the scale of tastiness (e.g. *bland, tasty, delicious*).

→ Add modifiers for the words on each scale, e.g. *very, a bit, quite, rather, absolutely* for weather temperature adjectives. Make it clear which ones tend to modify words in which bands of the scale. For example, *absolutely* tends to modify only adjectives at the extremes of a scale whereas *a bit* tends not to fit extremes at all.

→ When reviewing, or elaborating a previously introduced topic area, or eliciting language to go on a new scale, elicit basic words from less proficient students. Save the more difficult questions (about specific words, modifiers, connotations, etc.) and the intersecting scales for more proficient students.

TESTING

→ Use scales in diagnosing the level of a new class by spot-checking the size and refinement of their productive vocabularies. First draw a scale on the board (or write on a test sheet) and put the two basic polar words on. Explain the limitations of the topic area (e.g. *weather* temperature only). Then elicit additions to the scale from the group.

→ Present students with empty scales and a jumbled list of words belonging on it. Students then have to write the words at their proper location on the scale. Students could also be asked to mark words that have been wrongly included on a scale (e.g. *luke-warm* on a scale of weather words).

→ At higher levels, ask students to add notes about connotations to (some of the) words on their scales (e.g. *blazing hot*: 'because of strong, bright sunlight'.

VARIATIONS

1 A variant of the polar scale is the stairstep, as in Figure 23.

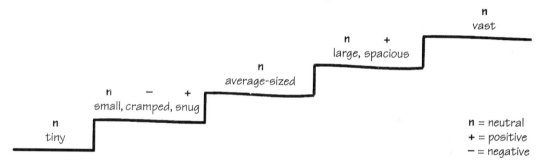

Figure 23 Size of rooms

2 Tree diagrams are particularly good for showing the relationships among nouns and, to a lesser extent, verbs. It can be useful to add other information in note or sketch form (see Fig. 24).

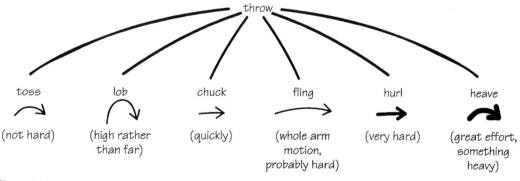

Figure 24

A variant of the tree diagram is the 'spiderweb', 'spoke' or 'hydra' diagram in which the branches extend in all directions (see Underhill 1980). An example of this is shown in Figure 25.

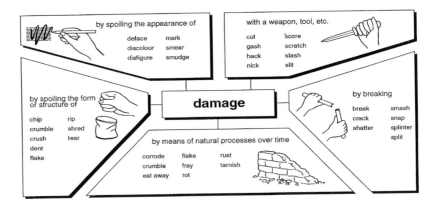

Figure 25

Longman Dictionary of Contemporary English

7.4

LEVEL
Any

TIME
5–15 minutes+

MATERIALS
To start off, 3 or 4 specimens of something you have several or more of at home

FOCUS
Building vocabulary; learning more about each other; getting a feeling for the range of what there is to say about a small number of objects

SMALL COLLECTIONS

Introducing the thread (at elementary level)

1 Bring in anything of which you have three or four specimens, for instance: sweaters, earrings, fridge magnets, baskets, fishing lures, saws. Pass the items around for close inspection.

2 The class brainstorms ways these things are the same, for example, about a sweater: two arms, no buttons, made of wool, a head hole.

3 The class brainstorms ways they are different, for example: blue v green, large v medium, thick v thin material, plain v striped, acrylic v wool, size 12 v size 14 (this might be on the labels), washable in hot water (ditto).

4 To review, one student describes one of the things (not necessarily in complete sentences) while *not* looking at it. When this student has finished, another student points to the item they think has just been described.

From lesson to lesson

→ Encourage higher-level students to come up with a greater variety of similarities and differences. If you get the feeling everyone knows the words that other students are contributing, add a few yourself, for example: *striped* v *plain*, *smooth* v *ribbed*.

→ Students, in turn, bring in anything of which they have three or four – spectacles, beer mats, etc. Students take on the role of teacher and lead the activity as in Steps 1–4. Lower-level students prepare their presentations in advance and check them with you before giving them.

→ Students give some of the history of the items in their collections. For example, where they got each item from, whether and why they like them.

→ At home, students write descriptions of their collections; encourage them to include sketches, diagrams and lists of the ways in which the items are similar or different. They hand these descriptions in. Check them and either type them up (with mistakes edited out) and hand them back, or suggest changes for them to make.

→ Move on to collections of intangibles. For example, outside class, students note down different sounds that people say when, for example, they're surprised, when they drop something, when they hoist a small child up in the air, when they're on the phone listening to someone talking steadily, when they feel a sudden physical pain. If students are in their own country, they can note down what people say in their mother tongue and ask you what the 'translations' are. If in an English-speaking country, they can demonstrate the sounds they've learned to the class. (The notation they use can be based on their own script or they can guess at a spelling in English; all they need to bring to class is a close enough approximation for you to be able to provide refinements.) Interestingly, in some countries people make *sounds* while in others they *say* something. For example, if startled, native speakers of English might say 'Uhhh!' or 'Oh!'. Japanese, however, are likely to say, 'Bikkuri sh'ta!', which means 'Surprised!'.

CHAPTER 8

Learning about oneself and others

Many of us allow a special time for 'getting acquainted' activities when we first meet our students. As we and our students all meet each other from lesson to lesson, we do of course continue to learn odds and ends about each other, no matter how the class is run. What we are advocating in this chapter, however, is that you set aside time quite regularly to actively promote the process of participants finding out about each other. One reason for this is that pair, group and even whole class work may remain dull, perfunctory and overly language focused unless students can get beyond superficial acquaintance with each other. Try supplementing the threads in this chapter with activities from, for example, Moskowitz (1978), and Davis and Rinvolucri (1990), or even with sessions of Community Language Learning (Stevick 1980 and Richards and Rogers 1986).

A sub-theme of this chapter, especially evident in threads 8.2–8.4, is building into your lessons a band of threads that each involves an individual student giving a talk or making a presentation to someone else, most often to the whole class. Specifically, this chapter offers ways of:

- starting at the shallow end so that students can develop the necessary confidence
- building fluency and presentation skills from lesson to lesson
- enhancing class interest through variety of format and topic.

HOT SEAT

The basic idea of *Hot seat* is that a student sits in a chair answering questions fired by the rest of the group. We have noticed, however, several other activities that build in a gradual and interesting way towards the dynamic and adrenalising *Hot seat* finale. This lesson band works by inviting a different student each time to be the one you all learn about that lesson, but by allowing the student to choose whether to bring in a picture or use any of the other options presented below.

Preparation

Find a portrait the size of an A4 sheet or bigger. (Magazines are good sources.) Try to avoid faces of professional models; choose characterful faces instead. Mount your picture on stiff card. Get a sheet of plain paper and cut out an oval just big enough to cover the key features of the face. Attach the oval to the picture, perhaps with a paper clip at the top. The activity will develop somewhat differently depending on whether you choose a person known or unknown to the person who speaks on behalf of this person (see below).

Introducing the thread (at beginner level)

1 Place one chair in front of and facing the class. Rest your picture on the seat. Let's suppose it is of a person unknown to everyone in the class. Prop it up against the back of the chair so that everyone can see it clearly. In big classes, pass it around. No peeping under the paper 'mask' allowed! They can't see the face but only hair, ears, neck, shoulders, necklace, shirt, etc.
2 Give students time to prepare questions to this unknown person. Either you or one of your students will answer for this person. If you decide on the latter, give this student (the 'answerer') an opportunity to go off in a corner of the room and peek under the paper covering. The class must not see the hidden face, though.

  The 'answerer' needs to imagine what the person is like, their biographical details, home, family, daily routine and so on so that they can start to feel what it would be like to *be* that person.
3 The answerer sits in the chair either resting the picture upright on their lap, or holding it up to hide their own face. Students ask their questions. The answerer answers *for* the head (i.e. *in role*, using *I* not *she/he*). For example, a student might ask, 'How old are you?' The answerer might say, '102!' or 'I'm a 102!' or 'Too personal'. (At higher levels they might reply 'I'd rather not say' or 'You tell me first how old you are.')

  At beginner level, you can help answerers prepare (while the rest of the class are thinking up and perhaps writing down questions). For example, you can ask what the answerer has decided about the

8.1

LEVEL
Any

TIME
5 minutes, a bit longer first time

MATERIALS
For introducing the thread at beginner level: a reasonably good-sized picture of someone's head and face; some stiff backing paper; an oval of paper large enough to cover the main features of the face; a paper clip

FOCUS
For students
The person in the hot seat practises answering, evading or returning questions; the other students practise phrasing questions

For you
Listening to what students can and cannot do in forming questions and answers; having time to make notes, write praise/correction slips

picture, reformulate this, and write it down to guide the student during the question and answer phase. For example, if the student says, 'I think it, woman, India, very old' you might write this down as 'I'm a woman. I'm Indian. I live in India. I'm very old.'

Or, again at beginner level, you can write answers to likely questions on the back of the picture (but *not* the questions!).

4 After the question and answer phase, ask pairs to recap on all the answers they remember. Go from pair to pair and check how much they remember. If there are big gaps from pair to pair, ask different pairs to call out what they remember.

5 The answerer shows the picture. Ask everyone to write a sentence or two about the person interviewed, in class or for homework.

VARIATIONS

If the person in the picture is well known, at lower levels you can help students prepare, perhaps a day in advance.

1 Ask the answerer to write down the answers she or he expects to give; ask other students to prepare questions, as for a formal interview. Just before you start the question and answer session, swiftly move around the class checking written work and offering suggestions on how to polish language.

2 Or, give the answerer a short paragraph to read about the person in the picture so that they can be well prepared.

From lesson to lesson

→ Students bring in pictures of interesting-looking people they would like to answer for.

→ Do 'empty chair' role plays. The class imagines that someone is sitting in a vacant chair. One student imagines a particular person and answers for them. This can be a fictitious person (an ideal boss or employee, etc.) or a real one (the answerer's boss, neighbour, etc.).

   If you think some of your students might find this a bit unsettling you can:

   • either ask people to answer for a pet (this works well with younger students)

   • or ask them to answer for a favourite car or house (this works well with older students).

→ Specialise in different language areas, e.g.:

   • refusing to answer questions. Perhaps give less proficient students useful phrases on slips of paper, for instance, *That's too personal, I'm not going to answer that, No comment, That's none of your business, What!?, What a cheek!, I might tell you later . . .*

   • deflecting/avoiding questions: *That's an interesting question. I've never thought about it. What do you think?* or *How would you answer that question?*

- answering like a politician, that is, answering a question that wasn't asked.
- asking questions in different ways:
  - simple and direct: *What's your name?*
  - like a frosty bureaucrat: *Name? Age? Daily routine?*
  - with elaborate lead-ins: *Would you mind if I asked your name?*
  - as incomplete statements with rising intonation: *Your name is . . ?*
  - as if the answer was known once but has temporarily been forgotten: *Your name again, was . . .?*
  - as if the person being interrogated was an animal: *What's your habitat? Do you have a dwelling? What sort? How is it constructed?*
- responding to answers: *Thanks, That's interesting, Gosh!, Really?, Why do you say that?, Hmmm* (with interest).

→ Students take notes on the interviews and write them up as if for a magazine or gossip column.

→ Instead of students being asked questions, give them a rigidly fixed length of time, e.g. two minutes, during which they can talk about anything they like. Call the activity 'Student time' or something else besides *Hot seat.* Give them a set phrase for introducing their talk (e.g. *I'm going to tell you about . . .*) and for indicating the end (e.g. *OK. That's all!*). (Perhaps write these on the board.) Ask them to follow with a request for questions (e.g. *Any questions?*) and give them a phrase for yielding the floor (e.g. *If there are no more questions, I'll hand over to . . .*).

→ Each student speaker is introduced by another student. Give introducers a skeleton to work from, e.g.: *The speaker today / Our next speaker is someone we have known for . . . We all know her/him as a person who . . . So, without further ado, I'll hand over to . . .*

ACKNOWLEDGEMENTS

We learned the idea of the picture with the covered face from Mario Rinvolucri, the idea of the 'hot seat' from Ruth Kasarda, and the idea of empty chair role plays comes to us from John Morgan (in Lindstromberg 1990, pp. 42–3).

8.2

LEVEL
Elementary+

TIME
A few minutes+

MATERIALS
An object from home

FOCUS
Building vocabulary; allowing each student to hold the floor for a while; seeing some interesting things; learning more about each other

BRING IN AN OBJECT

This thread and the one that follows (8.3) continue on from 8.1. In 8.1 the student, though in the hot seat, is often in the role of responder to questions. But here and in 8.3, the student in the hot seat has to initiate more, to give actual presentations.

This thread is an example of the familiar school activity 'Show and Tell'.

Preparation

Choose an interesting object from home – something with a story. Bring it to class.

Introducing the thread

Describe your object. Say where you got it and why you like it. Leave some space for students to ask questions.

From lesson to lesson

From then on, students take turns bringing in objects and presenting them as you did. Each presenter prepares the vocabulary they need to describe their object, give details of purchase and say why they like it. They may ask you to help before or during their talk. You, or a student, can 'store' new vocabulary on posters or everyone can set aside a page in their notebook under such headings as:

● size: *It's tiny / medium-sized / miniature*, etc.
● texture: *It's fluffy / slick / soft*, etc.
● where from: *from my granny / won it in a raffle*, etc.
● because: *It reminds me of / I've had it for ages*, etc.

VARIATION
Students bring in photos or books.

MY ROOM, MY WINDOW

Introducing the thread

1 Draw a plan of one of your own favourite rooms at home (e.g. Fig. 26).
2 Bring it to class and give a presentation based on your plan.

8.3

LEVEL
Elementary+

TIME
5–10 minutes

FOCUS
Building vocabulary; practising free oral communication; letting each student hold the floor for a while; getting students more interested in each other's worlds and ways of seeing things

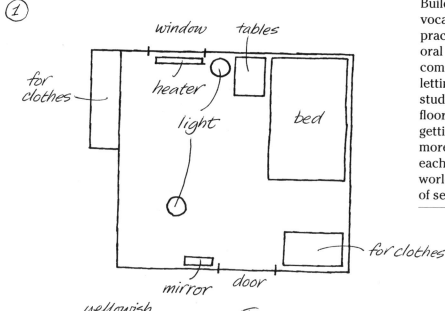

(1)
window | tables
for clothes
heater
light
bed
for clothes
mirror | door

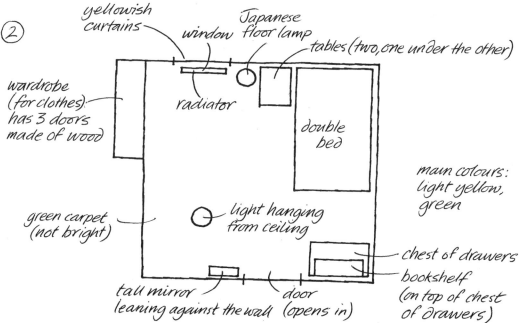

(2)
yellowish curtains
window | Japanese floor lamp
tables (two, one under the other)
wardrobe (for clothes) has 3 doors made of wood
radiator
double bed
main colours: light yellow, green
green carpet (not bright)
light hanging from ceiling
chest of drawers
bookshelf (on top of chest of drawers)
tall mirror leaning against the wall
door (opens in)

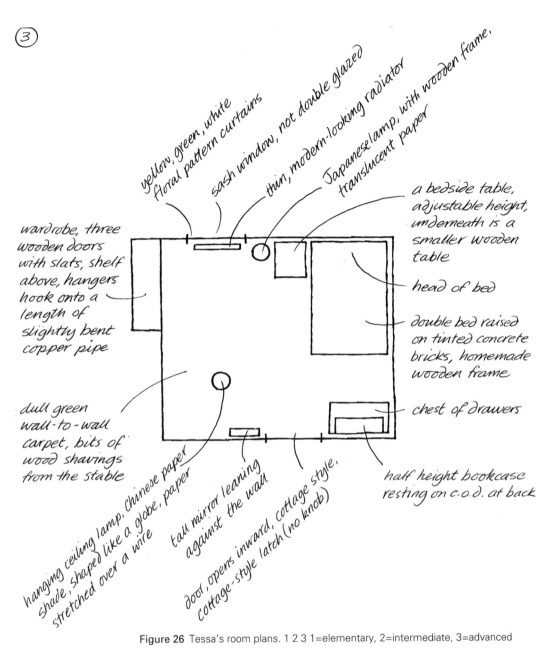

③

yellow, green, white floral pattern curtains

sash window, not double glazed

thin, modern-looking radiator

Japanese lamp, with wooden frame, translucent paper

a bedside table, adjustable height, underneath is a smaller wooden table

head of bed

double bed raised on tinted concrete bricks, homemade wooden frame

chest of drawers

half height bookcase resting on c.o.d. at back

wardrobe, three wooden doors with slats, shelf above, hangers hook onto a length of slightly bent copper pipe

dull green wall-to-wall carpet, bits of wood shavings from the stable

hanging ceiling lamp, Chinese paper shade, shaped like a globe, paper stretched over a wire

tall mirror leaning against the wall

door, opens inward, cottage style, cottage-style latch (no knob)

Figure 26 Tessa's room plans. 1 2 3 1=elementary, 2=intermediate, 3=advanced

2 One by one, on different days, students who want to do so bring in
their own room plans and present them to the class.
  If you are teaching students who have come from abroad:
- make sure they understand that *home* means their real home,
  not their host family home. (This should make the activity more
  interesting.)
- if they have all come from the same school or company and
  know each other pretty well, it might be more interesting if
  instead they do describe their room in the host family's house.

If your class is taking place in your students' home town, you might,
for the sake of interest, offer them the option of drawing the plan of
a room in a different town (or village, or time of life, etc.) provided
they have a very clear recollection of it.

From lesson to lesson

→ Tell your class what you can see from a window in your favourite
  room. Then students, in pairs, tell each other what they can see
  from some window. (Mingle and help with vocabulary.) Students
  then report to the class, mentioning only the things their partner
  sees from her/his window which they would never see from
  theirs.

→ Ask your class how they really, *really* know they're home when
  they've come back from a long trip. For example, describe a dis-
  tinctive person you often see around your house or in your town
  and who you see nowhere else. Thus, from time to time we see a
  neighbour trundling garden clippings into the old paddock
  behind his garage across the street. To us, he seems most dis-
  tinctly English in every respect and we cannot imagine a Scot or
  a Welshman looking like him, let alone someone from abroad. For
  Tessa, seeing him going about his business is a reminder that she
  is really home after a trip abroad.

  For homework, ask your students to think about a person who
  strongly suggests 'home' to them. Say they can make labelled
  sketches if they want and that the person should not be someone
  who actually lives *in* their house. Students present their thoughts
  (and sketches) one by one over a few days.

ACKNOWLEDGEMENT
The variation about the person who reminds you of home comes from
Sophie and Mario Rinvolucri.

8.4

LEVEL
Any

TIME
3–5 minutes

MATERIALS
None

FOCUS
Speed in sketching the visual gist of people and objects; getting students used to being up in front of the class, used to using the board

ON THE BOARD, SKETCH IT QUICK!

You may want to introduce this short, amusing thread shortly after beginning the 'hot seat' activities described in 8.1–8.3. It's particularly useful as a brief change-of-pace activity, or as a boundary marker between classroom activities that have nothing to do with each other. It's best used with adults who have been together for several lessons already. If you doubt the maturity of your class (e.g. if they are teenagers), ask them to draw objects and anonymous stick figures rather than particular people in the class.

Introducing the thread

1 Depending on the size of your board, ask one or more students to stand near it and get ready to draw. If you have enough board space for the whole class, so much the better.
2 Tell the 'artist/s' to take as much time as they need, up to a couple of minutes, to draw a portrait of you (i.e. neck up only), either front on or side view. If anyone says they can't draw, say 'That's OK, the worse the better' or some such thing.
3 Allow time for the drawings to be commented on, admired, laughed at.
4 Now say that the artist/s must draw the same portrait in twelve seconds. Repeat with deadlines first of ten, then eight, then six seconds. (Very often the last portrait will be the best.)

From lesson to lesson

→ Students (again at the board) draw themselves however they like: in portrait, head to toe, and from different angles (front, side, back, top).
→ Set other relatively simple subjects for drawing, e.g. a straight-backed chair, a stick figure running, a stick figure going up/down-stairs, someone cooking.

COMMENT
Usually, such a high proportion of a class will be poor or mediocre at drawing that no one will stand out as being terribly below average. Anyway, it's not awfully embarrassing to be poor at drawing, so it's not usually difficult to get good participation from everyone. Additionally, quick informal board drawing actually is learnable. Some students get noticeably better at it very quickly, as if they just needed to pick up a trick or two by seeing how colleagues draw. Other students, of course, turn out to be quite unusually good at drawing. This is always interesting for you and the others to discover.

Teacher themes: ways to variety

INTRODUCTION

In Part 2 the focus moves on from what students can learn to what teachers can learn. The central concern is that section of a lesson plan headed 'What do *I* aim to work on in this lesson/over the next few lessons?' The title, *Teacher themes*, is our term for threads of personal experimentation in a teacher's classroom practice. These threads can help you avoid burn out by keeping you interested, learning and professionally alive. They are concerned with the management of *your* learning rather than with students' learning.

Before you jump in and start changing things in your teaching, it might be a good idea to sit down and take stock for a few minutes. Usually we only have time to think about our teaching when we're busy planning our next lesson. It's actually quite a luxury for a teacher to sit down and try to remember what kind of teacher they wanted to be when they started off.

Gathering information

Here are three quick, easy ways of beginning to think about the kind of teacher you are or want to be. You can take a few minutes to do each activity separately or, if you begin to get engrossed, do more than one.

1 Write down, in random array, adjectives to describe the atmosphere you most like to have in your classroom. For example, *calm, busy, quiet, noisy, attentive, silent, democratic,* etc. Don't worry if some of them are contradictory; in different moods and on different days you might well want different atmospheres.

2 a List the sounds you most like to hear during a lesson. For example, music, silence, one student at a time speaking carefully, people's footfalls, taped dialogues of authentic English, the bell at the end of the lesson, students whispering in pairs, etc.

   b List the sounds you least like to hear during a lesson. For example, yourself shouting, students shouting, the scrape of chairs, a knock on the door, the jingle on the coursebook tape that comes between the exercises, etc.

3 Review your basic tenets about classroom language learning. Write about ten, of any type, that are as fundamental as possible. For example: 'Students should have a language rich environment' or 'A teacher must be able to spot discipline problems early and nip them in the bud, so that there is never an undignified open confrontation with a student.'

You can use these reflective exercises to generally get into the subject of teacher experimentation. One insight you may come to is that what you want and what you have are very different things! A good way to find out what you have is to ask your students. In order to compare your and your students' perceptions you can ask them to write down:

1 adjectives *they* would use to describe the atmosphere of your/their classroom

2 what sounds they hear in class

3 what they think your main beliefs about teaching and learning are.

Obviously, the thoroughness with which you can compare perceptions depends on your students' level in the target language or whether you share their mother tongue. But even elementary students know and can choose between words like *quiet* and *noisy*.

Although you probably won't have the time or resources for any large-scale data gathering, there are still many ways open to you of gaining different views on what goes on in your classroom. Here are a few more:

- Tape yourself, then listen and reflect. Make notes on such things as:
  a how much 'wait time' you tend to allow after asking a question or giving instructions
  b how often you echo good answers, or fail to acknowledge a student contribution, or answer a different question than was asked, or ask open reasoning questions (e.g. 'Why . . .?', 'How . . .?')
  c how often each student speaks or how often any student initiates an exchange with you or anyone else in the room
  d which students don't participate.

Transcribe an interesting part of the recording and analyse the discourse and interaction.

- Video yourself and watch the tape, either while filling out an observation schedule or while trying (without many preconceptions) to spot something of potential importance. You might ask a colleague to view your tape with you.
- Invite a colleague into your class and ask them to use an observation schedule of your choice, or one designed by you.
- Interview your students.
- Talk to your colleagues about specific issues; ask for suggestions.
- Introspect. Perhaps keep a teaching diary.
- Encourage students to keep learning diaries. Ask if you can read parts of them.

- Analyse student homework.
- Take notes during your lessons (perhaps while students are writing, reading or listening to a tape) or shortly afterwards.

(See past issues of *The Teacher Trainer* for more on many of these options.)

Using the information

NEW AREAS OF SIGNIFICANCE

Apart from using the information simply to find out about your teaching and to become more confident by seeing or hearing yourself at work, you can employ it in other ways. Let's suppose you've just tape recorded three successive lessons with a particular class, or have followed one or more of the options just mentioned. Try to approach the data you have gained without prior expectation and just see what it throws up. It's quite possible that things will appear significant to you that were never considered significant on your training course(s).

For example, it might suddenly occur to you that as the teacher, you have the right to start, join in with, and stop any conversation that takes place in your classroom. Do you give yourself the right to remain silent? Observations and questions such as these might lead you to reflect on the issue of *students'* rights. Do *students* in your classes have the right to start, join in with, and stop any conversation? Do they have the right to remain silent? To move around the room when they want? To write on the board when they want? To use dictionaries, of whatever kind they like?

Or, you may notice that some student voices are never heard on the tapes. Or that you never see any homework from certain students. This might lead you to try to discover whether these students are making more, less, or the same amount of progress as the others, or whether in fact there is little correlation between participation and progress.

Or, it may occur to you that in your classroom different things are getting explained in many different ways by different people, while, on your training course, explaining may have come up as a topic only in terms of teachers explaining grammar and vocabulary to students in a small set of ways. You might decide, though, that the ability to give and understand explanations, on the parts of both teachers *and* students, is central to teaching and learning.

In other words, by looking open-mindedly at the data you gain from investigating your teaching, you may find new areas of significance emerging for you.

WHAT ARE YOUR PATTERNS?

You might notice from your data that your classroom behaviour has recurring patterns or is downright repetitive in some ways. It would be very odd, in fact, if this were not so. For example, you might notice that you always use the same few ways of stopping pair- and group-work. Or you might notice that your lessons have roughly the same shape or the same number and type of phases each time. You may notice that in part this leads to a pleasant and predictable rhythm for students. But you may decide that you and your students could do with a few changes.

JUMPING STRAIGHT IN WITH DOING SOMETHING DIFFERENT

Some teachers might not fancy sitting down and thinking about their teaching or gathering information about it before trying something new. They will prefer to try something new and reflect later. Just jumping right in can be an interesting way of working too, especially if you choose an area which figures in current Second Language Acquisition (SLA) classroom process research. Once you've tried out something new in the area, reading articles and research reports can become much more interesting and fruitful. Some areas you might consider are:

- different types of classroom discourse
- teacher discourse (e.g. use of factual v reasoning questions)
- responding to errors
- differences between pedagogic and natural talk
- learner communication strategies.

(For more on SLA research, including reading leads, see Ellis 1990 as well as the periodic 'state of the art' surveys of recent SLA research in the journal *Language Teaching*, e.g. July 1993.)

Conclusion

The basic aims of Part 2 are to exemplify what we mean by 'teacher themes' and also to stimulate you to:

- deepen your interest in teaching and learning generally
- reflect on how you teach
- consider how well your teaching suits your students
- confirm what's good and effective in your teaching
- develop your teaching in particular areas through reflection and experimentation
- read up in the areas of language teaching/learning that take on significance for you
- talk to others who are interested in developing *their* teaching too
- raise your confidence.

In Chapters 9, 10 and 11 we have chosen themes that can fit in with any of the three main ways of approaching experimentation which we have discussed under the heading *Using the information*.

In Chapter 9, we take an area of central significance to teaching and learning, but one which sometimes gets a bit lost on topic-packed teacher training courses, namely *explaining*. We explore different

ways of explaining, together with their advantages and disadvantages, as a way of helping reflection on your normal practice.

In Chapter 10, we look at some *teacher patterns* – small-, medium-
and large-scale – and discuss how you can get your patterns to evolve
in directions that you desire.

In Chapter 11, we look at an area currently under investigation by
SLA researchers: *responding to errors*.

In addition to its central aim of stimulating teacher development,
Part 2 has the additional aim of enabling teachers to take greater
advantage of the 'Hawthorne effect'. (This name derives from a
famous study on worker productivity carried out at the Western
Electric plant in Hawthorne, Illinois in the 1930s.) The gist of this
effect is that experimentation with working conditions tends to raise
productivity *by itself*, regardless of which variables in the conditions
experimenters happen to change. The way it works seems to be this:
people become inspirited both by the increased variety of experience
that is involved and by the clear signs that someone is showing an
interest in them. Your *interest* in your students (as signalled by your
experimentation) has the potential to enliven them and improve their
performance. The *variety* entailed in this experimentation can enliven
not only them but you as well and so deepen your interest in, and
commitment to, your work.

Finally, because the subject matter of Part 2 is different from that of
Part 1, a slightly different format is necessary. Each chapter is therefore presented as a menu of questions and options. In general, variables such as time, level of learner, material and focus are either not
applicable or are made clear in the description of individual options,
so there are no special headings for these variables in Part 2.

READING
- Approaches to classroom research: Hopkins 1985.
- Gaining information from observing and the management of
  observation: Wragg 1993.

CHAPTER 9

Explaining

From looking at the information you have gathered about what goes on in your classroom you may notice new areas of significance in language teaching/learning. This might happen, for instance, when you think back a lesson you have just taught or while you're listening to an observer feeding back on one of your classes. In this chapter we look at one such example of an area of significance: *explaining*. Although you may have thought about how you are going to explain the meaning of a word or the difference between two tenses, you may not have had the chance to consider 'explaining' as a central area of concern in both teaching and learning at all times in a lesson.

We divide our discussion in the *From lesson to lesson* section (below) into seven main questions. As you read through these and their various optional answers, you will probably start quite naturally to think about *your own* practice in the area of 'explaining'. If you're not sure just what your normal practice is, then find out by video or sound taping yourself or by asking a friend to sit in on a couple of your classes. (See the introduction to Part 2 for more ideas about how to gather information.) Then try to introduce some of the variations into your lessons, little by little. Thus, if you normally explain by talking, try drawing. If students normally ask you for explanations, find ways to encourage them to ask each other. If you normally stop at one explanation, try to get two from different sources. If words are normally explained in a *pre*-vocabulary slot, leave the explaining till students request explanations, whenever that might be. If you normally explain *ad lib*, prepare explanations before class. Plan to include all the main stages of a good explanation (see below). If you notice that you often leave a stage out, e.g. 'identifying the problem' or 'checking the outcome of the explanation', then deliberately try to include it while planning/teaching subsequent lessons.

By varying your current practice in ways like these and thinking about when and why certain methods and techniques seem effective, you will inevitably widen the range of teaching moves that you are comfortable with in the area of explaining (or whatever other area you choose to work on). Your broadened repertoire of methods and techniques will increase your ability to work helpfully with people who differ greatly in learning style.

Some people are very gifted at giving understanding to others. Others have to work at it. For example, adults who have many times in their lives given street directions may remain quite poor at helping others to find their way. Teachers, however, should not allow themselves to fossilise at a low level of competence at explaining. Gomes de Matos points out that if learners have the right to receive decent explanations, then teachers have the right to be trained as effective explainers (1990: 12). Yet, from what we have seen of materials for TESOL teacher training and teacher development, broad development of explaining skills is a neglected aim. There is a fair amount of emphasis on a small set of techniques such as use of context, pictures, realia and diagrams (e.g. time lines) in clarifying the meaning and use of grammatical structures and vocabulary (see *Acknowledgement/Reading* below for materials containing these). Beyond this, there doesn't seem to be much. Explaining, then, seems like an area ripe for development on the part of TESOL teachers and teacher trainers generally. In Thread 3.3, *Teaching definition skills*, we have already looked in detail at strategies that help students to improve their ability to explain lexical meanings to each other. But the issue of explaining has enough further aspects for it to warrant another space in this book.

From lesson to lesson

WHO OR WHAT EXPLAINS?
The different sources of an explanation are:
- a student explains to a student
- the explanation comes from a wall chart, dictionary, coursebook, or some other resource such as someone outside of class
- you explain.

Requests for explanations come from various sources too, especially: students, teachers, coursebooks and other published resources.

STUDENT-TO-STUDENT EXPLANATIONS
→ Teachers can encourage student-to-student explanations by asking, e.g. 'Do you/Does anyone know why . . .?', 'Can anyone help?' Sometimes, however, just leaving a bit of silence is enough to elicit explanations.

For:
- Students quite often understand what another student doesn't understand, better than you.
- It can be quite irritating for students when a teacher explains something they already know.
- It's very good for a student's morale to successfully explain something.
- Explaining can provide an opportunity to *use* language.
- Students may well contribute something you didn't know.
- It's efficient to get other people helping you out with explanations during pair- and groupwork since you can't be everywhere.

Against:
- No one may know the answer and so you will have used up a few seconds to no effect.
- Language problems may cause some unintelligibility and generally slow things down.
- As with most options, the overuse of this one can become tiresome to some students.

STUDENTS GO TO ANOTHER SOURCE
→ Encourage student use of other sources of explanation. Keep reference materials handy e.g.: bi- and monolingual dictionaries, the Longman *Language Activator*, the *Longman Dictionary of English Language and Culture*, student grammar books, single volume encyclopedias.

For: This is a way of turning speaking time for you into reading time for all of your students, followed by speaking time when they report the explanations they've found. It's also a good way of familiarising students with target language and other reference materials.
→ Encourage students to ask different people and to come back and report the explanations they were given.

For: They hear different voices and probably also get extra speaking time.
Against: You never know what wacky explanations they'll get! (Sometimes it's a good idea to be specific about who to ask.)

STUDENTS ASK YOU FOR AN EXPLANATION
Students often request explanations simply by asking, 'Why . . .?' or 'How . . .?' but what happens next is not always equally straightforward. Some teachers – who knows, maybe the majority – come into the profession feeling rather insecure about their knowledge of some content area like grammar. A very small minority of these also imagine that classrooms are prone to contain devious students intent on unmasking them personally as an ignoramus. The ability of teachers to react effectively to student-to-teacher questions is clouded by other (doubtless more common) factors too. Whatever the reason, teachers can fail to notice or fail to acknowledge substantial numbers of questions.

→ It does seem that some teachers are better than others at dealing with and listening to more than one person at once. How good are you? Find out by bringing a cassette recorder to class, primed for recording. Set it going at the beginning of an elicitation, brainstorm or some other activity where more than one student is likely to be trying to get your attention at once. Listen to the recording soon after the class. Are there many voices that you never heard at the time? Any unacknowledged questions?

WHAT IS EXPLAINED?

Most methods of language teaching (but not all) see the teacher as the main decider of what gets explained. In fact, whoever determines the course content (teacher, administrator, coursebook author . . .) is involved, since what needs explaining is a reflection of what is to be covered on the course (as well as how clearly the content is presented, whether it is presented at the right time for students to make sense of it and whether it is remembered or forgotten).

Interestingly, there may be elements of course content which both teachers and students tacitly decide not to touch with a barge pole, doubtless owing to previous experience on both sides of ineffective, inaccurate explanations. The English article system is a good example here.

WHEN ARE THINGS EXPLAINED?

BEFORE

→ If you expect certain explanations to be asked for, you can prepare for them in advance by trying to imagine your students' state of knowledge about an issue that might come up in class and preparing one or more explanations. Tape record and listen to your explanation/s before or after class. Ask yourself:
  ● Would you understand if you were one of your students?
  ● Have you given enough detail or examples?
  ● Have you said so much that students lose sight of the core of your explanation?
  ● Do you repeat certain points too often?
  ● Do you paraphrase any particularly difficult vocabulary?
  ● Ask someone else, maybe a non-teacher, to listen to your recording and tell you what *they* think.
  ● Could you do it all better with a picture, a gesture, etc.?

For: If you jump right in with an explanation, you can save the time otherwise taken up by a student asking for it.

Against: You run the risk of explaining something people already know or of interrupting them while they're thinking of something else.

ON REQUEST

Of course, you or anyone else in the room can try to explain immediately after being asked.

For: An explanation given in the context of a stated need may be more intently listened to, better understood and better remembered than one that is given at some other time.

Against: Sometimes people need time to think before they can explain well.

SOME TIME LATER

If asked for an explanation, you may decide to postpone giving one for a while. Perhaps a student has asked 'privately' (i.e. during pair- or groupwork) and you think the explanation is something everyone needs to hear. Maybe you suspect that the inquirer or some other student will think of a good explanation if you wait for a while. Or, perhaps you don't have an explanation ready and you want to have time to think.

→ Perhaps you would even like to postpone an explanation until the next lesson. If so, try this:

1 Take a deep breath. (This seems to help!)

2 Say, 'That's a very good question. I'd like to think about it. I'll tell you what I think next lesson.'

3 Don't forget. Write yourself a reminder of who asked and what the question was.

4 Before the next class do some reading and thinking about the problem and/or ask colleagues what they think.

5 Get back to the student in writing or orally.

→ Perhaps you think the inquirer is not ready for the fullest explanation you could give. It may be that you believe that certain elements of language are learned in a natural order (e.g. the Simple Past well before the article system). Or, possibly you think your fullest explanation would simply not be understood, would not be remembered or would not hold the asker's attention to its end. One option is to be frank. Give a preliminary explanation and say, 'There is more, but I will tell you later.'

→ Sometimes it is clear that only some members of the class are interested in having a certain point explained.

1 Give those not interested a task which will take them a few minutes to complete. For example, ask them to individually make a list of at least six words they remember from the last lesson. Then they should compare in pairs. If they disagree about meanings, they should check in a dictionary.

2 Explain to the rest.

→ If only one or two students want a certain point explained, ask them to see you during break or after class.

→ Postpone the explanation but don't give it yourself. Suggest sources of an explanation and assign someone to track them down and report.

HOW LONG SHOULD THE EXPLANATION BE?

Knowing when to stop explaining isn't easy.

→ Force yourself to stop talking the instant you've finished giving the gist of your explanation. Then wait a bit, look and listen.

For: If you allow silence at the end of a (foreshortened) explanation, you provide your students with the opportunity to think and ask questions and you provide yourself with time to look carefully for signs of incomprehension and/or time to think of checking questions.

SHOULD YOU REPEAT AN EXPLANATION OR NOT?

Students can determine this by saying they still don't understand just after an explanation has been given. Teachers can determine this on the basis of a judgement about whether the first explanation has been effective. But should a second or third explanation be substantially the same as the first?

→ If your initial explanation hasn't had the desired effect, check first of all to see if anyone remembers hearing it! You might say, 'On Monday, second period, about ten minutes after class started, I explained something. On the board, right there, there was a picture of a motorcycle going over a bridge. There was a little river. Who remembers what I talked about? Just give me a short sentence or just a word.'

→ Ask students to try to reconstruct the explanation in small groups, in English or in their mother tongue. Groups then report to the class. Invite them to use the board or any other handy aids to support what they say.

→ If you feel another explanation is needed from you, radically rework your original. Use different aids and examples. Restructure the order in which you tackle different points. Do anything you can think of to come at the matter from a different angle. Perhaps explain in less depth than before, or in more.

For: Why repeat an explanation that didn't work in the first place?

WHAT IS A GOOD EXPLANATION?

No matter who does the explaining or when the explaining happens, it's obviously important that the explanation be a good one. As it happens, there has been surprisingly little written, at least in English, about the features of effective explanations. Much of what *has* been written recently comes from George Brown of Reading University and various co-authors (e.g. Brown 1982, Brown and Atkins 1988: 19–25 and Brown and Wragg 1993). Here we summarise key points emerging from their work:

1 Good explanations are clear. There is evidence that clarity in verbal explanation is fostered when explainers:
   - have clear voices
   - use 'signposts' to show direction and purpose ('There are two important things you need to know about . . .')
   - structure their explanations clearly
   - clearly mark the boundaries of steps and sub-topics
   - highlight the really important elements
   - establish links among the parts of an explanation and between the explanation and the explainees' experience
   - repeat and paraphrase key elements of the explanation
   - reduce the use of words like *it*, *this* and *here* and instead use more full noun phrases or very clear gestures (as when pointing to a part of a time line).

2 Good explanations are interesting. Interest can be enhanced by using gesture, different intonation, eye contact, appropriate examples and analogies, and a mix of 'modes of explaining' (i.e. narrative, anecdotal and conceptual). Arousal of intellectual curiosity is an important factor which teachers can call into play through setting problems and puzzles, asking questions and stating or eliciting analogies. Humour is important too.

3 Good explanations show empathy with students and involve them somehow. For example, they may incorporate and acknowledge student contributions (e.g. 'You remember what Tomoko said about . . .? Well, we see the same thing when . . .'). Or they may include times when students explain, show or re-explain things to each other.

4 Explanations should also be persuasive; for this the explainer needs to show an interest in the topic as well.

5 The stages of a good explanation are as follows:
   a Consideration of the problem
   b Deciding what kind of explanation will suit whoever has asked for the explanation
   c The explanation
   d Checking the outcome.

HOW CAN THINGS BE EXPLAINED?

→ Go beyond speech and the written word. Use realia, gestures, sounds or pictures. Use a range of graphic techniques such as colour coding. Use different presentation aids (e.g. OHP, the board, Cuisenaire rods). Question your colleagues specifically about ways in which they explain non-verbally or support verbal explanations with non-verbal materials or techniques.

→ Cater to different learning styles.
   • Help those who think analogically to see parallels between new information and what they already know.
   • Give those who learn by trial and error plenty of feedback on their work as they do it rather than explain to them before they start.
   • Help those who like to understand systems from the ground up by explaining elements and inter-relationships. Diagrammatic overviews can be especially helpful to these students.
   • Other students seem to learn by imitation. They need plenty of examples rather than explanation.

(See Rogers 1986 for more information).

→ While speaking, monitor your speech for potentially unfamiliar vocabulary since you may not want to add to the number of question marks hovering over students' heads. If you do hear a doubtful word or idiom fall out of your mouth, follow it with a paraphrase.

→ Experiment with introducing/eliciting examples *before* discussion of general principles rather than afterwards, and vice versa. There is some evidence that proceeding from examples to principles is helpful, especially when students know very little about the area in question. Proceeding the other way around, from principles to examples, seems most apt for students who are on more familiar territory. (Brown and Atkins 1988: 23).

→ Mentally group any examples that come up in your planning or in class into one of the following three categories:

Positive examples These are ones which fit whatever rule, principle or explanation that is being considered.

Negative examples These show the limits of the application of a rule, etc. as when you say, for instance, 'What we're *not* talking about here are sentences where . . .'.

Rogue examples These are examples which at first sight seem neither clearly in nor clearly out of the limits of an explanation or which seem to contradict it in some way. Approaching rogue examples as puzzles can lead to explanations being refined, broadened or rejected. Brown and Atkins (1988: 24) recommend that examples generally be considered in the following order: positive, negative, rogue.

→ Give two radically different explanations. For example, when explaining the use of *some* v *any*, give the traditional EFL view that *any* occurs mainly in questions and negatives while *some* occurs in positive statements and questions where something is offered. Say there is another view. *Some* means 'more than zero, less than all'. *Not any* is usually for 'zero' ('There isn't any beer'). *Any* shows 'open choice' ('Anyone can come'). *Some* can also mean we have a particular individual or group in mind ('Someone did it'); *any* can mean that we don't ('Anyone who can speak ten languages is pretty smart'). Leave it up to your students which explanations to go by.

For:

• This seems particularly appropriate when the experts themselves are in dispute and you have no way of knowing who is really right. Or when you think each explanation might suit different members of your class. Even if you do have strong views yourself, there are advantages in allowing students to form their own opinions about the plausibility of competing explanations.

• This may foster their independence in learning.

Against:

Some students dislike not getting a straight clear answer from their teacher. So be prepared.

→ Give a vague but thought-provoking explanation based on analogy, proverb, parable or gnomic characterisation, e.g.:

Imagine a quiet, windless pond. A stone falls into the middle of it. If the ripples are still there, use the Present Perfect. Use the Simple Past when they are gone. The bigger the stone, the longer the ripples last. This is a general rule even if you're not talking about ponds but about, perhaps, news.

The indefinite article is for classifying. The direct article is for identifying.

How do we use *on the other hand*? Imagine I tell you my opinion about a certain topic. When I do that, it's like I take an iron bar and bend it in one direction. Then I say, 'On the other hand . . . blah, blah, blah'. When I do that, I bend the bar back towards being straight again.

Resist the temptation to elaborate. If anyone has questions say something like, 'I'll take questions on this next lesson. Before that, could you look at these examples.'
For:

It may do no harm to set students' minds off in a search for significance in an assertion that is less than crystal clear. This is a method much favoured by Zen masters. (By the way, the explanation above of *a/the* is current among theoretical linguists.) Explaining in this way won't suit everyone, but then what does?

HOW CAN YOU TELL IF YOUR EXPLANATION IS EFFECTIVE?

A vital part of developing your effectiveness as an explainer is to check the effectiveness of the different kinds of explanations that you give.

- When explaining, gather feedback of different kinds as you go along. Look at students' faces; ask questions; give checking tasks and quizzes; set students off explaining to each other and monitor what they say and do.
- Gather and consider data on your explaining in the form of sound or video tapes, or transcripts.
- Ask students to evaluate the effectiveness of (1) your choices of what to explain in the first place and (2) the different techniques and strategies that you use.
- Directly observe and then reflect on the explanations your students offer to each other and those of other teachers.
- Seek comment and insight from your colleagues, director of studies, head of training, etc. about your explanations.
- Watch videos, listen to sound tapes or read transcripts of other people at work explaining things.
- Ask other teachers, 'How do you explain . . .?', 'How do you give students the opportunity to learn key concepts?'

ACKNOWLEDGEMENTS/READING
Gomes de Matos 1990 and Moore-Flossie and Lourdes 1992 started us off thinking about explanation in the classroom. Gower and Walters 1983 (pp. 65–78) discuss use of context and concept questions in presenting verb structures. Allsop 1983 contains lots of time lines. Brown 1982, Rogers 1986, and Wragg and Brown 1993 are good introductions to the subject of explanation generally.

CHAPTER 10

Changing patterns

As mentioned in the introduction to Part 2, you might start to become aware of recurring patterns in your classroom, as follows:

teacher patterns such as only ever using the same two pictures, seeming to always be doing activities that involve you talking, having teaching aims that never include any work on discourse, always seeming to be explaining things and never getting students to use the target language for real communication, giving lessons that involve rather aimless groupwork, things always seeming to go slower than desired, etc.

students' patterns such as what they do when they come into the room, where they sit, who they sit with, who talks the least, what they do when you come into the room, how they communicate with each other, who participates the most (women or men? younger or older students?), the conditions under which they initiate conversation, who supports you, and so on.

Once you've established what normally happens in your classroom, i.e. what the patterns or 'rules' are, you can decide to change patterns or break rules. Even tiny changes involving very little preparation or thinking time can introduce new feelings of interest and freshness into your lessons. In this chapter, we look at two areas where patterns are easily set up and quite easily changed. The first example of this non-threatening, small-scale kind of change involves the use of classroom space. The second is about getting people's attention.

CLASSROOM SPACE

The use of classroom space is about where you and your students are during your lessons, whether people are sitting or standing, where you all tend to be in relation to each other, and so on.

From lesson to lesson

→ Think about your classroom. Draw diagrams of where people were during a couple of your lessons, i.e. where they sat, stood and walked. (Perhaps you can fill in these maps during pair- and groupwork.) You may, for example, discover the following:

Your students walk . . .
- when entering and leaving the classroom
- occasionally to the front of the class to write on the board or to do a brief role play
- otherwise not at all.

They sit . . .
- most of the time
- in hard chairs
- in a horseshoe arrangement, without desks or tables
- in the same places most of the time even though you have not assigned seats.

You stand . . .
- most of the time
- usually near the board, mainly to the right.

You walk . . .
- back and forth in front of the board
- within the curve of the horseshoe.

You sit . . .
- almost never.
→ Think about why you and your students have got into these patterns. Sometimes you may not need to reflect. We know one school where the management forbids teachers *ever* to sit down. But sometimes the answers are harder to put your finger on.
  - Have you unconsciously modelled yourself on teachers you've observed, either as a student or a colleague?
  - Do you just stick with the arrangement of chairs you always find when you walk into the class?
  - Is there an immovable fixture that's caused you to take on certain habits? Perhaps you never stand to the left of the board because there's a fixed shelf there. (Does it serve a purpose? Perhaps you can persuade the management to have it removed.) Perhaps you always station yourself in one part of the class because that's where the power point is or a window you like to look out of.
  - Do you sit down a lot because you're tired? Do you roam around a lot because you're restless? Or do you do what you do for a clear pedagogical purpose? What is it?
→ For the area you've chosen to focus on, imagine doing something very different, indeed, the opposite if there seems to be an opposite. For example:
  - *What if you had students sitting around small tables (three or four to a table) so that students at one table all faced each other rather than all facing forward towards the board?*
    Would you be going against a school tradition? A national tradition? What specific changes would this entail in your

lessons? How would you keep the noise level down or get everyone's attention when you needed to? Would you have fewer plenary activities, use the board or OHP less, do less drilling, include more writing phases, spend more or less time speaking at close quarters to individual students? And so on.

- *What if you sometimes grouped your students in teams near the board for some sort of competitive game?*
  Would this go against their established routine? Would they feel uneasy about this or enjoy the change? Would you be running the risk of losing control? How do you know? Would you want to hover near them giving them instructions or would you feel comfortable taking one of the vacated seats and letting them get on with things?

- *What if you sat down more often/most of the time/always?*
  Would you do less correction of spoken errors? Less monitoring of students' writing while in progress? Fewer activities involving students standing up and moving about? Less writing on the board? Would the students near the front be less loomed over?

- *What if you left the room for minutes on end?*
  Would your students run riot? Would they feel that they could do their assigned work, a discussion task perhaps, with more self-expression? How responsible for their own learning do you think your students feel with you always in the room?

- *What if you sometimes came late on purpose?*
  Are there threads that students could set up and manage for themselves?
  And so on.

→ Make a short list of desiderata for your class. For example, 'Students talk more and I talk less', 'Students move around more and stay more awake and involved', 'Students consult me more one to one, when they want to'. Think of ways you can achieve these changes. Begin to conduct small experiments in breaking out of the patterns you've identified so that you can move towards the way you want things to be. For example, if you want to establish the feeling that the whole room belongs to everybody equally:

- Exchange places with students sometimes. Let individual students stand at the board and present an idea for a minute or two. You take their seat.
- Set students off working and leave the room for a minute or two.
- Get students working in groups at the board. Sit in the back of the room and keep quiet.
- Clear a large space somewhere and set students off on an activity where they stand up and mill around talking to each other. (For ideas here, see especially Hadfield 1984, 1987, and 1990.)

- Roam around while students are writing. Perhaps stop and sit down for a couple of minutes here and there in different parts of the room.

Or, to take another example, suppose you have a class in the West composed mainly of people from less rich countries. Perhaps they seem ill at ease sitting in a horseshoe or sitting in groups around scattered tables. Do you never have them sit in rows at desks or tables? Make an exception. Is there a change for the better?

GETTING EVERYONE'S ATTENTION

Our second example of an area for small-scale change of patterns is getting your students' attention both in routine situations – for instance, before you give instructions and when you want to bring an activity to a halt – and in 'emergencies', such as when you realise you've given the wrong handouts to half the class.

Getting students' attention can be a problem for many teachers, especially in large or noisy classes. There are plenty of classes which, after a while, don't respond at all promptly when their teacher claps her/his hands and calls out, 'Now listen everybody!' In any case, such overt and stereotypical teacherish behaviour can cause stereotypical behaviour in the class. Introducing an element of novelty can be far more effective (and satisfying to you) than just calling out your plea for attention at ever-increasing volume.

Some of the options described below give students a degree of responsibility for establishing quiet and a mood of attention. This allows different voices to be heard (and yours to be rested). If it comes down to it, students can often be rather good at being disciplinarians of each other.

From lesson to lesson

BASIC TECHNIQUES
→ Vary when you end tasks. Stop when the quickest have finished, when all have finished, when fifty per cent have finished, etc.
→ If you're about to move on to an activity which has nothing to do with the one before, be crystal clear about it ('Now for something completely different!').
→ If staging a string of related activities, make the transition from one activity to another more organic.
- One way to do this is to give instructions for more than one activity at a time. For example, rather than just say, 'Write three sentences about X' say, 'Write three sentences about X. Then, when you're finished, look around to see if anyone else looks finished. If so, pair up and compare answers. Then go

back to your seats.' It's a good idea to note this on the board too in case students forget what they're supposed to do after the first task. You can tell how people are progressing simply by watching them shift from one activity to another. If anyone appears to have forgotten what you said, you can remind them individually by pointing to the board rather than interrupting the work of the class as a whole.

PREPARING TO STOP

→ Warn students of activity changes. While students are working, write notes on the board ('Five minutes left') or stroll around and speak directly to individuals or groups.

→ Before a task, in your instructions, tell students what to do when they finish and what signal to expect from you ('When you finish, open your notebooks and review new words from yesterday. Then, when I tap on the board, we'll do something new').

→ Establish a system whereby you hold up your hand to signal 'stop' and students hold up theirs as they notice you or others with their hands up and stop talking. (We learned this from Lew Barnett.)

→ Ask students to suggest starting and stopping signals.

→ Nominate a student to give the signals.

→ With the class, agree a signal they will give *you* when they've finished (e.g. turn over their papers, begin chatting to a neighbour).

→ Circulate, finding out where people are in their work. Ask individuals/groups how much more time they need. Judge the stopping time accordingly.

→ After giving instructions but before starting the activity, ask the class how much time they think they need. Let a student be timekeeper.

GETTING ATTENTION

→ Use different means.

- Switch the lights off and on.
- Jingle an Indian bell.
- Shake a tambourine or use a whistle or a party noisemaker.
- Drum your fingers on a metal wastepaper bin.
- Write on the board (e.g. 'Could you finish now and wait for me to say something?').
- Hold up a sign (e.g. 'Let's do something new').
- Turn some music on/off/up/down.
- Hand out notes (e.g. 'Shin, could you finish talking now and get ready for some new instructions? P.S. Pass this note on.').
- Whisper to individuals (e.g. 'Please tell your neighbours we're stopping now.').
- Hand out reading matter; as soon as students get it they will tend to stop talking and begin to read it.

→ Get your noisiest student to come to the front of the class and get everyone's attention.

→ Suppose groupwork has been in progress and there is one student who ignores all signals to stop talking. If you don't want to be heavy handed in getting this person's attention, try this. Move near to a student who isn't saying much and is near the talker. Using the talker's name, ask this person what the talker is on about. Ask for more and more details, repeatedly using the talker's name. It's a very unusual person who can keep talking when they keep overhearing their name being used. (We learned this from Gottfried Rohmer.)

READING

John Fanselow has written a wonderfully fat and detailed book on the subject of breaking rules, (1987). For some variations on what we've said here, see Woodward 1989. An area related to *Getting attention* is 'Dividing your class up into pairs or small groups'. For ideas on this see Woodward 1991, p. 54.

CHAPTER 11

Responding to errors

As mentioned in the introduction to Part 2, one way of getting interested enough to do reading on second language acquisition is to jump straight in and experiment in an area which is currently receiving a lot of attention from researchers. By the time you've tried out some experiments of your own, you'll probably find it really interesting to read how other people have fared in their classroom-based or more formal investigations. In the introduction to Part 2 we also mentioned several areas that could be ripe for this sort of work. In this chapter we choose one to deal with: 'responding to errors'.

In working with hundreds of pre-service teachers, we've noticed a tendency among many of those who are *working in their own language* to overlook some written errors and almost all spoken errors. The reasons for this are probably that these new teachers are either so concerned with getting through their (observed) lessons that they haven't got any extra attention to devote to the details of students' grammar, wording and pronunciation, or they get so caught up with the communication itself that they forget to notice its form. When native-speaker teachers do develop to the point where they actually begin to notice *how* students speak and write, another tendency frequently comes to the fore: drifting into the use of a very small set of familiar ways of reacting to errors.

Non-native speaker teachers, on the other hand, seem generally to get involved in error correction right from the beginning but also often work with a very small set of well-known reaction types.

These common ways of reacting to errors apparently stem from two sources:
- popular lore about how language teachers are supposed to react to errors
- the reaction patterns of any language teachers one had oneself.

The latter must be an especially strong source of habit for non-native speaker teachers since they are doubtless likely to take on board teacher behaviour that figured in their own successful learning of the language.

The commonest ways of reacting to errors seem to rest on these four beliefs:
- correction of errors can be helpful
- correction works best if the teacher does it
- for best effect, correction of spoken errors should be instant
- it is most efficient to correct spoken errors by voice and written ones with coloured ink.

Each of these beliefs can lead to helpful classroom practice. However, other beliefs lead to different and potentially equally helpful classroom practice. Trying out different classroom practices can change beliefs.

There are many facets of the subject 'responding to errors'. Here are some that you might like to consider:

What do students actually say or write and are there any deviations from target language norms?
Learners can have trouble in any of the following areas of communication:

- pronunciation, e.g. any of the following aspects of pronunciation: stress placement at word, phrase or sentence level; rhythm; intonation; articulation of individual sounds; liaison between words, e.g. *lookin there* (natural) / *look in there* (stilted or angry); dropping of sounds, e.g. *givim time* (colloquial) / *give him time* (formal or angry); assimilation, e.g. *goobbye* (colloquial) / *good bye* (formal or angry)
- syntax, e.g. errors in word order or use of auxiliaries/articles
- morphology, e.g. omission or malformation of prefixes, suffixes, verb/noun endings; mistakes with internal changes such as *ring, rang, rung*
- vocabulary, e.g. faulty choice of lexis including unnatural collocation
- register, e.g. use of formal wording in an informal situation, or adoption of a colloquial pronunciation feature in a formal setting
- style, e.g. overuse of a particular lexical item or unnatural use of a grammatico-semantic feature such as the historical present tense
- proxemics, e.g. standing too close to a speech partner
- gesture, e.g. snapping fingers when calling a waiter, peremptorily beckoning the teacher whenever help is needed
- eye contact, e.g. avoidance of it
- cultural appropriacy, e.g. overuse of respect forms like *madam* and *sir*, prefixing first names with *Miss*, *Mrs* and *Mr*, or asking someone how much they earn
- discourse, e.g. overuse of discourse-ordering items like *and then*
- use of humour, e.g. making culture-specific jokes.

What teachers don't react to
With so many areas involved, teachers obviously have to establish priorities about what to react to. The way we were trained may also give us habits in what we react to. For example, we may never discuss student problems of voice tone, gesture or eye contact. When going over students' writing, we may correct within sentences but forget to discuss what makes a good paragraph, a good narrative, etc. We may remember to praise in class but on homework mark only what's wrong. We may be unable to see that while a particular student's vocabulary is extensive, it's also rather ornate and formal. How many of us know whether we react thoroughly and consistently to the errors that *students* want to work on?

How are errors viewed?

Are errors viewed primarily as a problem of form, as communication breakdowns in need of repair, as evidence of the state of a learner's interlanguage, or as an evaluation problem (e.g. 'How many marks should I take off for this?')?

How are students alerted to error?
- By lack of approval?
- By disapproval?
- By silence?
- By a request to try again?
- By the teacher turning to another student?
- By teacher correction whether by voice, by gesture, or in writing on the board, on flashcards or on slips of paper, etc.?

When is feedback given?
- Never?
- Immediately after the error has been made?
- Later/Much later?
- During all phases of a lesson / During some?
- At different frequencies during different activities?

Is the feedback noticed by students?

Is the feedback understood?

Is the feedback taken up in subsequent work done by students?
In other words, does the kind of feedback you give your students actually work?

Is error treatment uniform?
For example, are the same errors corrected for all students? Are the same errors corrected in all parts of the lesson?

How many errors are caused by the teacher?
- Giving an over-simplified rule about use?
- Over-teaching a particular item (leading perhaps to students over-using it)?
- Being unclear?

Undoubtedly, there will be other aspects of reacting to errors that interest you. For example, how much chance do students have to express themselves and therefore to deviate from the target language norms?

Below we suggest some fairly small-scale threads of experimentation in the area of responding to errors.

From lesson to lesson

LEARNING TO GIVE STUDENTS SPACE
Most teachers probably have a few unconscious patterns of behaviour which diminish students' opportunity to think, to contribute or

even to finish what they might have begun to say. Any programme you undertake to alter your patterns of reaction to spoken errors depends on your developing an awareness of any such patterns that you have. For one thing, there are unconscious teacher patterns which probably promote error by forcing students to speak under pressure in great haste. Or you may have ones which keep *you* under pressure to speak and so prevent you from paying adequate attention to what students say, and indeed provide little chance for students to speak at all. Two common patterns of this sort are (a) habitual echoing of student responses and (b) not leaving enough wait time after you or a student has said something. Below, we describe each of these patterns in turn and offer suggestions about how to change them if you wish.

→ *Echoing and how to control it* Many teachers routinely echo student contributions, especially when eliciting. That is, if a student contributes an answer or a suggestion (with falling, statement-like intonation), the teacher repeats it (with the same intonation). Here are typical examples:

Teacher: Can you tell me some things that are red?
Student: Some apples.
Teacher: Some apples.
Student: Kazuo's shirt.
Teacher: Kazuo's shirt.
etc.

When asked why they do this, teachers tend to say it's to 'reinforce the language' (whatever that means), to make sure all the other students hear what's said, to correct pronunciation. Deeper motives for echoing might be:

- a desire, born of nervousness, to take firm possession of centre stage, to keep wresting back conversational initiative
- fear of silence
- pure habit.

One reason for thinking *these* are the real, if unconscious, motives, is that many teachers who regularly echo are unaware that they do so until they hear themselves on tape or read a transcript of one of their lessons.

Let's look at some of the disadvantages to echoing:

- Students have less incentive to speak up or improve their pronunciation for the benefit of the rest of the class if they know that the teacher can generally be counted on to do it for them.
- It may be difficult for students to know what to make of an echo. Does it mean the original utterance was wrong in some way? Or that it was right but the teacher was just providing positive reinforcement, or echoing out of nervousness?
- If the teacher keeps grabbing the floor, it just becomes harder for student-to-student interaction to happen.

- Habitual echoing will tend to prevent you from making some other, clearer response to a student contribution such as error correction or a normal, conversational reaction like 'Really?', 'Mmmm', 'Then what happened?', etc.

Giving up echoing is as difficult as giving up smoking. It takes iron self-discipline and a real desire for change. Try replacing your echoes with other verbal responses such as 'Yes!' or 'Interesting' or use gestures such as nodding or giving thumbs up. Echoing is something you should be able to do or not do when you want to. If you have self-control in this area, you will be better able to take advantage of those times when you want students to speak to each other, not to you, and when you want to step aside and just listen.

→ *Wait time* This sometimes means the time a teacher leaves after asking a question. Here, though, what we have in mind is mainly the time you wait before responding when spoken to by a student. In order to get a good pace going or to involve the maximum number of students, it's tempting to react very quickly to student contributions. One possible disadvantage of this is that you don't leave yourself enough time to hear and reflect on what students say. To work on this, identify a period of time in a forthcoming lesson during which students will be speaking to you or to the whole class. (Many of the threads in Part 1 involve such times, e.g. 8.1–8.3). Decide that during this time you will always delay your response a certain number of seconds (three or four, say). It can be amazing how much you notice during these lengthened pauses about what students have said, how they have said it and what they probably meant by it. Rowe 1978, in a study of 800 primary school lessons, found that teachers tended to wait a second or less for students to respond to questions. She found, after persuading teachers to wait just three seconds, not only after teacher-to-student questions but also after student responses, that the following occurred:
- Students spoke longer. In particular, they were more forthcoming with evidence, inferences and guesses
- The number of unelicited student contributions increased
- There were fewer failures to respond
- Students spoke to each other more
- Students asked more questions
- Slower learning students spoke more
- There were fewer discipline problems

ESTABLISHING GROUND RULES
→ Clearly signal which activities you will correct in and which you will not correct in. One way to do this is to make a reversible sign like an 'Open/Closed' shop sign, only this one says 'Accuracy' in

red on one side and 'Fluency' in green on the other. Explain what these terms mean. Say or elicit why proficiency in both areas is desirable. Explain that when the 'Accuracy' sign is showing, there will be error correction and when the 'Fluency' sign is showing, there won't be. Students and teacher can negotiate the percentage of time given to the two different signs.

RECORDING AND CLASSIFYING OBSERVATIONS

As you leave students more room in which to speak, and get better at hearing what they say, you grow more open to information about your students' strengths and weaknesses. What can you do with this information so as to put it to best use?

→ In a notebook specially kept for this purpose, write a different student's name at the top of every other page. Use this notebook to record samples of students' language. In each lesson or part of a lesson, focus on one student in particular. Initially, just note down individual utterances, preferably verbatim.

Use your notes (a) when planning what to review or (b) in deciding which of the errors you've been hearing might be worth a response in the future, what kind of response this might be and from whom it might best come.

→ In particular lessons, concentrate on more than one student with respect to just one category of error (e.g. pronunciation) or sub-category (e.g. rhythm).

→ As the number of entries grows under each name, scan the entries and distill them into notes about the *categories* of error each student makes, e.g. 'Kyoko: often confuses word class / uses derivational endings wrongly, e.g. "She is very friendship".'

→ Record 'errors of avoidance', i.e. what students have encountered but never use. For example:

Elementary: Classroom language: Always says *Repeat, please* never *Again, please?*

Advanced: Uses ornate, formal discourse links such as *moreover*, but never uses more colloquial ones such as *on top of that* and *for another thing*.

→ *Students categorise and evaluate errors*
1 Give students a copy of a list of errors you have heard them make. (They can add to the list by looking through old assignments.)
2 They sort the errors into different categories such as 'errors I don't care if I make', 'I want to get this right', 'meaning changes', 'meaning doesn't change', 'word choice', 'register', 'tense' and so on. In a lower-level class, you might suggest categories to choose from. Higher level students might want to think of their own.
3 When the categorisations are finished, students compare them in groups. Listen in. Or, if you have assigned the categorisation as optional homework, ask those who have chosen to do it if you can see their work.

Discuss with students individually. Invite them to tell you one or two categories of error they would particularly like to work on in the near future. Guide them in distinguishing short term possibilities from long term ones. Note their choices, if any, in your notebook.

DELAYED RESPONSE

A major and especially interesting overall option in responding to errors is to provide or arrange for the provision of a delayed response.

For: In many cases an immediate response may be distracting or may not be adequately noticed. This is especially likely to be so when students are engrossed in *communicating*.

Below, we examine ways students can get delayed response to errors.

→ *Students give feedback about errors* Before pair- or groupwork, arrange for each pair or group to be listened to by a classmate. Tell the observers what to listen for. Observers simply make notes e.g. tally the number of well- and ill-formed occurrences of expressions of interest in what the other person was saying, or tick off items on a hand-out you give them (e.g. well-formed phrases relating to a situation pairs or groups are going to role play). After the pair- or group-work, the observers tell the students who were observed what they noted down.

→ *Correction slips* When students are speaking to the whole class (as in Threads 7.4, 8.1–8.3) or are working in groups, you can note errors on slips of paper that you hand back after the activity has finished, just before break or at the end of class (see Fig. 27). Either note down exactly what a student said and then add a correction afterwards or just write the error verbatim and ask the student to return the slip with the error corrected. In this last case, you keep the slip filed alphabetically by student name in a pack of similar slips. If in future the student makes the same or a related error, note this on the same slip as before and hand it back to the student again.

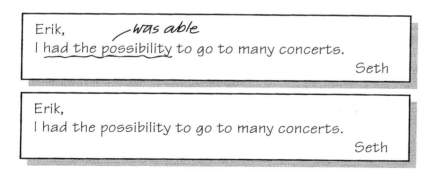

Figure 27 Two kinds of correction slip: (a) error plus correction and (b) error only

> Tomoko,
> You said this: "It'd been raining off and on all day."
> (Very natural English!)
>
> Seth
>
> P.S. Sorry your books got wet.

Figure 28 A positive feedback slip

Further variations: (a) Write 'positive feedback slips' as well (Fig. 28). (b) Use carbon paper when writing your slips. In this way you simultaneously furnish yourself with a record of what student language you have responded to. (c) If you ever have an observer in the room, ask *them* to do the correction slips. That way they can be of use to both you and your students.

→ *Discussion* Hold a post-activity or end-of-lesson discussion. For example, say what errors you heard or write them on the board. Displaying them on an OHP can be especially efficient, provided you have made your notes directly onto OHP transparency. Invite students to comment. (It's usually not necessary to say who made which mistake.) A variation is to include some examples of well-formed student speech too.

→ *Reformulation* When you 'reformulate' a piece of student language, you write or speak (e.g. onto a tape) a version of the piece which is as close as possible to the student's wording and intention but is in natural English. That is, the reformulation says what the student wrote or said but with errors corrected, style improved, register unified, etc.

This kind of feedback is particularly appropriate when you wish to deal with student errors and successes not one by one but *at the level of text*. A special plus point in the eyes of some students is that reformulation does not, in the case of written work, leave their original marked up and written on by you. Instead, they get their original back just as they handed it in. Additionally, they get your natural English version. They can then compare the two and make whatever notes or corrections on their original that they like, or none at all.

The basic procedure for reformulating spoken student language (easily adaptable to reformulating written language) is as follows:

1 Record whole passages of what one or more students say during a talk or a discussion.

2 Produce a written or tape-recorded reformulation. You can do this after class, during a break or in class while students are busy with, for example, a longish writing or reading task.

3 Hand out your reformulation(s). You can either:
   - highlight similarities and differences between the original and the reformulation,

or,

- simply allow time for the student(s) to read both versions and notice and ask about what they will. This option is most suitable if you think it theoretically dubious to suppose that a teacher can say exactly which elements of language a student is ready to learn at any given time.

A variation of the reformulation idea is not to provide students with direct reformulations of what they have said or written, but instead to provide written or recorded examples of native speakers saying or writing the same kinds of things for similar purposes. For example, if a student has given a short talk, they compare a recording or transcript of their talk with a recording or transcript of a native speaker giving a similar talk.

- *'Reformulation Dictation'* A drawback of reformulation from the teacher's point of view is that it can be time consuming, so much so that it can be impossible to provide reformulations of more than a few relatively short texts per day. A way for you to provide a limited amount of reformulation for more students at a time, is as follows:

1 While individual students are taking turns speaking before the whole class (e.g. when giving talks or doing role plays), note down one or two errors per student. Reformulate them, keeping track of who said what. Add in a few strikingly well-formed and creative student utterances as well.
2 Dictate the reformulations along with the unreformulated, correct utterances.
3 When the dictation is complete, ask students who, during the activity before the dictation, had said which of the items you dictated. Don't say what the original errors were unless specifically asked to.

Rationale: You emphasise the reformulations and original successes rather than the errors.

- *'Mistakes Dictation'*

1 Dictate a mix of correct and incorrect phrases/sentences you've noted down during recent classwork.
2 Either,
  a students write the correct and incorrect items on different parts of a sheet of paper (e.g. correct at the left and incorrect at the right)

or,

  b they write only the first letter of each word if the phrase/sentence is correct. If it's incorrect, they write it out in full but with the error corrected.
3 When checking (if you have used **b**), see if students can remember the full wording of the correct sentences.

(Adapted from Rinvolucri 1984, p. 89.)

→ *Student research* Give students materials in which they can research troublesome areas on their own: grammar books, short parallel mother-tongue or target-language texts, dictionaries, coursebooks other than ones being used in your class if these have better or simply different explanations, articles from easy-to-read journals like *English Today*, etc.

→ Whatever area you experiment in, read up on other people's work. (See especially Ellis 1990 for overviews and reading leads.) Also, it's a good idea to resist any temptation you might feel to generalise expansively or to proselytise on the basis of the kind of personal, small-scale investigations we have been talking about in this chapter and in Part 2 generally. However, if you are scientifically minded, pursuing your own teacher themes might well lead you on to research involving carefully-formulated hypotheses and rigorous testing procedures, use of control as well as experimental groups, consideration of broader and/or longitudinal samples, and employment of statistical analysis.

ACKNOWLEDGEMENTS/READING
Error correction in general: Bartram and Walton 1991 and Edge 1989
Correction of written errors: See also Cohen 1987
Delayed error correction: Rinvolucri 1984, pp. 18–19
Correction by student observers: Edge 1989, pp. 44–46
Reformulation: Wilberg 1985.

Afterword

'I don't think that if teachers are going to teach a grammar point, for example, that there's only *one* way that will work for that. There are a number of combinations depending on the teacher and what's happened before. In my own teaching, I'll often start with a free bit and then focus in on something. But whatever the trainees choose to do, if it seems to be working and they can say why they're doing it, then I'm happy. It's a bit of a dilemma really. You can't start with nothing and say, "It's OK, you can do *anything*!" They won't know where to start. You've got to give them *some* framework to start them off. But how much structure do you give before you start stifling their creativity? It's like wind-surfing. You start by learning lots of techniques and then when you can windsurf really well, you break out of all the frameworks and do other things. You need structure first to get started. Once you've started, you can break the rules and follow your own threads.'

(Sheelagh Deller, EFL teacher, trainer and author)

Many teachers plan in terms of blocks of content. Where does this way of working come from? First of all, from one's own experience as a student. Doubtless also from coursebooks, which seem almost invariably to demand block planning. Training courses must be influential too, and in a number of ways. Trainers working on part-time or full-time training courses, pre- or in-service, can impose their own ways of shaping lessons on their trainees by:

a what they show, i.e. the demonstration lessons they give
b what they preach, i.e. the models for lessons they offer on the course
c what they practise, i.e. how they structure their own input sessions
d what they plan, i.e. the teaching practice points they give out
e how they help, i.e. the lesson planning help they give, including format of plans, suggested starting points, suggestions for activities and ways to proceed
f the way they structure their observation of trainees, i.e. what they look for and what they see in the trainees' plans and teaching practice
g what homework they set, e.g. the lesson planning tasks they assign
h what they say in feedback
i how they judge, e.g. the overall grade

Our experience suggests that the cumulative effect of all these streams of influence can be *exceedingly* powerful, so powerful, in fact, that we recommend that trainers:

- develop awareness of their own normal attitudes and behaviour patterns in areas (a)–(i)
- expand their own repertoire of these patterns, e.g. by using not only blocks but also threads as ways of structuring courses. (The term *thread* is defined on pp. 7–10.)
- be accepting of trainees' attitudes and behaviour, e.g. by accepting a sequence of lessons that involves some use of threads rather than nothing but blocks.
- be accepting of the threads of personal development (as in Chapters 9–11) which trainees want to work on, and, if asked, try to suggest ways of working on these threads.

Finally, it seems clear that many trainers run courses sufficiently short in duration for them to decide that they have to drastically limit the number of lesson shapes they present to their trainees. We would like to express our hope, though, that trainers who do this will at least make it clear that there are many more lesson structures and structuring devices that also have sound claims to validity.

Bibliography

Allsop, J 1983 *Cassell's Students' English Grammar* Cassell
Bartram, M and Walton, R 1991 *Correction* LTP
Baudains, R and Baudains, M 1990 *Alternatives* Longman
Bowen, T and Marks, J 1992 *Sounds Improved* Longman
Brown, G 1982 *Explanations and Explaining* Methuen
Brown, G and Atkins, M 1988 *Effective Teaching in Higher Education* Methuen
Brown, G and Wragg, E 1993 *Explaining* Routledge
Cohen, A 1987 'Student processing of feedback on their compositions' in Wenden and Rubin (Eds) *Learner Strategies in Language Learning*, pp. 57–69 Prentice Hall
Cranmer, D and Laroy, C 1992 *Musical Openings* Longman
Crewe, W 1990 'The illogic of logical connectives' *ELT Journal* 44/4: 316–25
Davis, P and Rinovolucri, M 1990 *The Confidence Book* Longman
Edge, J 1989 *Error Correction* Longman
Ellis, R 1990 *Instructed Second Language Acquisition* Basil Blackwell
Fanselow, J 1987 *Breaking Rules* Longman
Frank, C and Rinvolucri, M 1992 *Grammar in Action Again* Prentice Hall
Gomes de Matos, F 1990 'Training teachers as explainers: a checklist' *The Teacher Trainer* vol 4/1: 12
Gower, R and Walters, S 1983 *Teaching Practice Handbook* Heinemann
Hadfield, J 1984 *Harraps Communication Games* Harraps
Hadfield, J 1987 *Advanced Communication Games* Nelson
Hadfield, J 1990 *Intermediate Communication Games* Nelson
Hopkins, D 1985 *A Teacher's Guide to Classroom Research* Open University Press
Krashen, S 1982 *Principles and Practice in Second Language Acquisition* Pergamon
Lindstromberg S, (Ed) 1990 *The Recipe Book* Longman
Longman Vocabulary Activator 1993 Longman
Maley, A and Duff, A 1975 *Sounds Interesting* CUP
Maley, A and Duff, A 1978 *Sounds Intriguing* CUP
Moore-Flossie, A and Lourdes, G 1992 'Explanations and explaining' *The Teacher Trainer vol* 6/3: 8–11
Morgan, J and Rinvolucri, M 1986 *Vocabulary* OUP
Moskowitz, G 1978 *Caring and Sharing in the Foreign Language Classroom* Newbury House
Murphey, T 1992 'Action logging: letting the students in on teacher reflection processes' *The Teacher Trainer* 6/2: 20–1
Peyton, J and Staton, J 1991 *Writing Our Lives: reflections on dialogue journal writing with adults learning English* Prentice Hall
Prabhu, N 1987 *Second Language Pedagogy* OUP

Richards, J and Rogers, T 1986 *Approaches and Methods in Language Teaching* CUP

Rinvolucri, M 1984 *Grammar Games* CUP

Rogers, A 1986 *Teaching Adults* Open University Press

Rowe, M 1978 *Teaching Science as Continuous Enquiry* McGraw-Hill

Stevick, E 1980 *Language Teaching: A Way and Ways* Newbury House

Stevick, E 1986 *Images and Options* CUP

Underhill, A 1980 *Use Your Dictionary* OUP

Wilberg, P 1985 *One to One* LTP

Woodward, T 1989 'Breaking rules' *Practical English Teaching* 9/4: 19.

Woodward, T 1991 *Models and Metaphors in Language Teacher Training* CUP

Wragg, E 1993 *An Introduction to Classroom Research* Routledge